The State of America's Black Colleges 2008

The State of America's Black Colleges 2008

Expanding Access, Ensuring Success, Promoting Global Competitiveness

A Publication of the National Association
for Equal Opportunity in Higher Education (NAFEO)

THE Beckham
PUBLICATIONS GROUP, INC.
SILVER SPRING

Copyright © 2008, NAFEO

All rights reserved. Printed in the United States.

No part of this publication may be reproduced or transmitted in any form or by any means, electronic or mechanical, including photocopy, recording or any information storage and retrieval system now known or to be invented, without permission in writing from the publisher, except by a reviewer who wishes to quote brief passages in connection with a review written for inclusion in a magazine, newspaper or broadcast.

Published in the United States by
Beckham Publications Group, Inc.
P.O. Box 4066, Silver Spring, MD 20914

ISBN: 978-0-9802380-4-4

ISBN: 0-9802380-4-8

ACKNOWLEDGMENTS

The editors would like to express their deepest gratitude to the NAFEO staff, the board of directors, and the members for their support and assistance in completing this publication. They would also like to thank Ms. Olivia Majesky-Pullman from Diverse: Issues in Higher Education for her invaluable assistance in data collection and analysis for the 2007 NAFEO Annual Membership Survey.

This publication was made possible through funding from the W.K. Kellogg Foundation and Lumina Foundation for Education.

The views expressed in this report are those of the author(s) and do not necessarily represent those of Lumina Foundation, its officers or employees.

Table of Contents

Acknowledgments v

About NAFEO xi

Introduction xi

Essays:

    Dr. William E. Spriggs 1
    Dr. William R. Harvey 7
    Dr. Trudie Kibbe Reed 16
    Dr. Everette J. Freeman 24
    Dr. Julianne Malveaux 30
    Dr. Wayne Watson 36
    Dr. George T. French, Jr. 42

Contributor Biographies 53

Appendices 59

Table of Land-Grant Colleges 111

Listing of Law Schools 112

Directory of Schools 113

NAFEO Board of Directors 133
NAFEO Staff... 134

THE EDITORS

Editor-in-Chief
Lezli Baskerville, Esq.

Managing Editor
LaNitra Walker Berger

Senior Research Editor
Lionel Smith

Charts
Lionel Smith

Publishing Consultant
The Beckham Publications Group, Inc.

ABOUT NAFEO

NAFEO was founded in 1969 by a group of HBCU presidents as the professional association of the presidents and chancellors of the nation's historically and predominantly black colleges and universities. NAFEO represents approximately 500,000 students and their families. NAFEO member institutions are public and private, two- and four-year, community, regional, national and international comprehensive research institutions, located in 25 states, the District of Columbia, the Virgin Islands and Brazil.

The mission of the association is as follows: to champion the interests of historically black colleges and universities (HBCUs) and predominantly black institutions (PBIs) with the executive, legislative, regulatory and judicial branches of federal and state government and with corporations, foundations, associations and non-governmental organizations; to provide services to NAFEO members; to build the capacity of HBCUs, their executives, administrators, faculty, staff and students; and to serve as an international voice and advocate for the preservation and enhancement of historically and predominantly black colleges and universities and for blacks in higher education.

From its inception, NAFEO has:

- Served as the liaison between the nation's HBCUs and various segments of society, including executive, legislative, regulatory and judicial branches of federal and state government and with corporations, foundations, associations and non-governmental organizations;
- Engaged in a variety of public policy, legislative, legal and advocacy activities on behalf of its members and partners;
- Sought and secured federal and private dollars for projects for its members;

- Designed and engaged its members in collaborative efforts to increase technology access; improve persistence and graduation rates; improve institutional performance; decrease health disparities in target service areas; increase capital and capacity; train new cohorts of HBCU presidents; strengthen the performance of member institution business and finance offices, enrollment services, student support services; preserve historic buildings; engage students in academic, athletic, business plan and other competitions; and educate the public about the importance of HBCUs;
- Convened a national legislative mobilization of NAFEO members and supporters annually. The conference brings together leaders in academia, government, corporate America and the private, non profit and philanthropic sectors, legislators, students and others for an exchange of information about blacks in higher education and equal educational opportunities; and
- Convened an annual Presidential Peer Seminar that brings together HBCU presidents and chancellors to provide them with information, inspiration, new skills and relationships to enhance their ability to serve at the helm of their institutions, meet the many demands of governance and better service their communities.

NAFEO's VISION

To be the leading and most respected advocate for historically and predominantly black colleges and universities, and for blacks in higher education by serving our members professionally, effectively, and efficiently.

INTRODUCTION

Lezli Baskerville, J.D.
President and CEO

The State of America's Black Colleges: Expanding Access, Ensuring Success, Promoting Global Competitiveness

Earlier this year, an article in Howard University's *Hilltop* student newspaper reported that black college students from around the country drove to South Carolina to support Senator Barack Obama's campaign to become the Democratic nominee for president. As the students prepared to canvas neighborhoods, they chanted, "Fired up and ready to go!"

Regardless of which candidate wins the election in November, this slogan echoes a sentiment that has existed on black college campuses for almost two centuries. Black colleges—their students, faculty, and presidents—have always been driven by their knowledge of the connection between scholarship and service.

NAFEO is pleased to release *The State of America's Black Colleges* at this time in which a movement for change is sweeping our nation, fuelled by young Americans, mostly students, whose discontent is being channeled into making a difference at ballot boxes across the country. This movement for change has brought the nation closer to realizing its egalitarian ideal, as we head toward the 2008 Party conventions this summer with an African-American male and a woman as the contenders for the Democratic nomination for the President of the United States—leader of the free world.

This movement for change has brought to the fore issues of poverty, health care, education access and success. It has brought the tremendous contributions of, continuing need for, and needs of the nation's Historically Black Colleges and Universities (HBCUs) to the center of the national public debate. The movement spurred at least one candidate for the presidency of the United

States of America to include in his or her platform a comprehensive plan for strengthening (HBCUs) and Minority-Serving Institutions (MSIs) and for financially rewarding institutions like HBCUs and MSIs that enroll and graduate disproportionate numbers of students of fewer financial means.

We dedicate this publication to the unprecedented numbers of students who are participating in a presidential campaign this year, especially those among the more than 300,000 enrolled at one of the nation's 103 HBCUs who are following in the tradition of the students of the Civil Rights Movement, those of the Voting Rights Movement, those of the Silver Rights Movement, students of the Black Power Movement, the Women's Rights Movement, the Anti-War Movement, the Free South Africa Movement, the Environmental Justice Movement, the Judicial Justice Movement, and all of the student-generated movements of the twentieth and twenty-first centuries, who are helping to move American closer to a more perfect union.

The State of America's Black Colleges is designed to provide the data that will dictate greater investments in HBCUs and in HBCU students like today's debating heroes, the progeny of the likes of Wiley College's debating heroes celebrated in the film, *The Great Debaters*; and like those who won the Ford Motor Company HBCU Business Classic, the Sallie Mae Fund Writers of Passage Writing Competition; the Honda All Star Academic Challenge, and those who protested racial injustice in Jena, Louisiana last year. The data herein demonstrate beyond peradventure that America's Black Colleges are producing graduates who are critical thinkers, civically engaged, prepared and ready to lead.

The state of America's black colleges is that they are strong and poised to get stronger with today's diverse cohort of black college presidents, administrators and faculty, and with greater investments by states, the federal government, corporations, foundations, and by the more than five million HBCU alumni. Black colleges are the nation's premiere equal educational opportunity institutions, graduating disproportionate numbers of black and low-income students each year. Although they represent approximately 3 percent of all institutions, HBCUs graduate approximately 30 percent of all African-American students and 40 percent of African-American students receiving a four-year degree in STEM (science, technology, engineering, and mathematics), and 50 percent of African-American teachers.

Despite these successes, in 2008 HBCUs will realize only modest increases in federal funding. In addition, black colleges continue to receive significantly less funding for research, facilities, and programs than their historically white counterparts. According to data from the National Science Foundation, for example, six of the top 20 predominantly white universities received more federal funds for research than 79 HBCUs combined.[1] The NSF report shows that despite a quantifiable record of success at educating African-American scientists and engineers, HBCUs continue receiving disproportionately fewer federal dollars. This pattern has created a barrier to black colleges remaining comparable and competitive with historically white institutions and must be reversed.

The State of America's Black Colleges provides a snapshot of the strengths, capabilities, and proposed growth areas of each of the nation's historically and predominantly black institutions. This year's theme is "Expanding Access, Ensuring Success, Promoting Global Competitiveness." In this inaugural edition of NAFEO's signature publication, you will see what our institutions are doing in each of these areas to guarantee that students at black colleges thrive.

The first section includes essays written by a distinguished group of NAFEO member presidents and faculty. These essays address some of the most important issues facing America's black colleges in 2008. William Spriggs, chair of the economics department at Howard University, opens with an analysis of the current trends in HBCU enrollment and graduation rates. William R. Harvey, president of Hampton University, reflects on his successful capital campaigns and the president's role in the crucial task of endowment building at black colleges. In her essay on strategic planning, Trudie Kibbe Reed, president of Bethune-Cookman University, provides strategies and best practices to guide college presidents in securing their institution's long-term stability. At a time when 50 percent of black men do not graduate from high school, Everette Freeman, president of Albany State University in Albany, Georgia, describes his institution's successful initiative to improve recruitment and retention rates among black males. Julianne Malveaux, president of Bennett College for Women, analyzes the crucial role that historically black women's colleges play in cultivating the next generation of black women leaders. In the wake of an increasing number of both natural disasters and man-made emergencies affecting college campuses, Wayne Watson, chancellor of the City Colleges of Chicago, discusses how community colleges play an essential role in supporting and rebuilding communities affected by disaster. Finally, George T. French, Jr. president of Miles College, writes about how he is preparing students on his campus to be competitive in the global economy.

As a resource for increasing academic/corporate/community partnerships and aiding foundations in providing funding for HBCUs and PBIs, *The State of America's Black Colleges* will be an invaluable reference tool. The appendices provide data and information on black colleges' tremendous value to their students, their communities, the nation, and the world. You will find one of the most comprehensive lists of majors and degrees offered by NAFEO members as well as listings of Centers of Excellence, data on faculty diversity at NAFEO institutions, special collections, distance learning courses offered, and the unique goods and services that black colleges produce for their communities and beyond.

As our nation confronts a host of political, social, and economic challenges at home and abroad, the need for America's black colleges has never been more acute. The United States is becoming more diverse, more technologically advanced, and more global in its outlook. Today's students must be trained to succeed as leaders. Building on their tradition of excellence in education, passion through service, and leadership through activism, America's black colleges continue to produce graduates who have proved that, against all odds, they are fired up and ready to go.

I invite you to learn more about NAFEO's members through *The State of America's Black Colleges*.

END NOTE

[1] Richard J. Bennof, "FY 2005 Federal S&E Obligations Reach Over 2,400 Academic and Nonprofit Institutions; Data Presented on Minority-Serving Institutions," *Info Brief,* National Science Foundation NSF 07-326 (revised), Directorate for Social, Behavioral, and Economic Sciences, October 2007.

Major Trends Facing Historically Black Colleges and Universities

Dr. William E. Spriggs

Chairman, Department of Economics, Howard University

Today, Historically Black Colleges and Universities (HBCUs) are positioned to benefit from changes in the makeup of America's college students. And, they continue to produce a disproportionate share of students in engineering and sciences, a vital element of the nation's preparedness for a globally competitive and technology-based economy. As a result of these beneficial changes, three trends are creating opportunities for HBCUs. The first trend is an increase in black students' college attendance, both absolutely and relative to all students; and a clear preference of black students to select colleges with high minority presence. But, to take full advantage of this positive trend, four-year HBCUs will have to find ways to successfully recruit the fast growing numbers of black students earning associate degrees. The second trend is an increase in college attendance by black women, and a third is increasing incomes for black households. This article highlights these three positive trends, and then examines challenges that also exist.

In 1994, slightly less than one million black students were enrolled in either two- or four- year undergraduate institutions, and made up 9.4 percent of America's college students. By 2004, roughly two million black students were enrolled in college, and made up 13 percent of college enrollment.[1] This means that black college attendance grew at a much faster rate than for all college students. Blacks were a rising share of the general population as well, increasing from 11.9 percent of the population in 1994 to 12.1 percent in 2004. But, while blacks were underrepresented among college students in 1994, being 9.4 percent of students but 11.9 percent of the population, by 2004, blacks were over-represented as college students, being 13 percent of students but only 12.1 percent of the population.[2] For the 2002–2003 academic year, blacks earned 11.4 percent of the associate's degrees and 8.7 percent of the baccalaureate degrees awarded by Title IV institutions, making blacks closely represented in relation to population size to the associate's degrees conferred, while still lagging among baccalaureate degrees.[3]

During the 1994 to 2004 period, the number of non-HBCU colleges that were at least 25 percent black, increased from 200 in 1984 to 622 in 2004.[4] Because of the increasing concentration of nonwhite students in either a minority-serving institution (a college where at least 25 percent of the students are nonwhite) or an HBCU, HBCUs face stiff competition for black students. Enrollment in HBCUs increased from 202,000 in 1984 to 270,000 in 2004, but enrollment at black-serving non-HBCU colleges went from 458,000 in 1984 to 1,491,000 by 2004.[5] While 63 percent of students enrolled in HBCUs attend public four-year colleges, 58.8 percent of students at the black-serving non-HBCUs are enrolled in public two-year colleges.[6] The biggest increase in black college enrollment is among students at two-year institutions. A challenge for HBCUs is to capture transfer students from this rapidly growing pool of black college students.

Black college students tend to choose colleges with high minority student presence. In 2004, 61 percent of black undergraduates attended a minority-serving institution: 13.4 percent attended a HBCU, 34.1 percent attended a black-serving non-HBCU institution, 10.4 percent attended a Hispanic serving institution, and the remainder were spread among Asian and Native American serving institutions. Among those attending public four-year colleges, 24 percent attended HBCUs and another 10 percent attended black-serving non-HBCU institutions.[7]

Public, four-year HBCUs are slightly more likely to recruit the traditional undergraduate, a student who enters college directly out of high school—74 percent of HBCU students in 2004—than is true for black college students at public four-year colleges nationally, 70 percent. They are also slightly more likely to recruit students with high school diplomas, 95.1 percent of HBCU students, than is true of black college students at public four-year colleges nationally, 94.2 percent. Additionally, they are more likely to have students who are full-time, full-year students, 61.1 percent of HBCU students, compared to black college students at public four-year colleges nationally, 52.9 percent.[8] Similar comparisons hold for private, not-for-profit four-year colleges, with HBCUs having 69.2 percent straight out of high school, compared to 58 percent for black students at private colleges nationally; and, 96.2 percent with high school diplomas, compared to 90.8 percent at private colleges nationally.[9] So, HBCUs are able to attract traditional college students as well as other institutions.

Both public and private four-year HBCUs have a greater share of black students majoring in engineering and science than is true nationally among black students, especially comparing HBCUs to nonminority-serving institutions. For instance, among public four-year colleges, 31.1 percent of black students at HBCUs are majors in engineering or science compared to 25.9 percent at nonminority-serving institutions.[10] Among private, not-for-profit, four-year schools, 27.0 percent of black students at HBCUs major in engineering and science compared to 20.8 percent at nonminority-serving institutions.[11] As a result, HBCUs are preparing their students for competitive futures.

The second trend is the growth in college attendance for black women. This is a positive factor for HBCUs because the children of black women with more than a bachelor's degree are about 28 percent more likely to attend a HBCU, all else equal.[12] The rapid growth in black women's college attendance puts their participation rate, the share of high school graduates age 18 to 24 enrolled in college, very close to that of white men.[13] This creates a potential growth in black students who would favor attending a HBCU.

A third positive trend is the growth in incomes for black households. Beginning in the late 1990s, for the first time, there was overlap between the incomes of black households who fell in the middle fifth of the black income distribution and the middle fifth for white family incomes. In 1995, the income range for white households in the middle of the income distribution was from a low of $37,382 to a high of $57,670 (in 2005 inflation adjusted dollars). For black households, incomes for the middle fifth of the income distribution ranged from a low of $22,201 to a high of $37,688. So, for the first time, blacks who were in the upper reaches of middle income for blacks were also in the middle of the white income distribution.[14]

The mean income for black households in the top five percent of the black income distribution have started to grow again since peaking in 1999 and falling through 2004, and similarly for the mean income of blacks in the top twenty percent of the black income distribution whose incomes also peaked in 1999 and fell through 2004.[15] Growth in incomes at the top of the black income distribution suggests room for growth in tuition revenue for HBCUs.

In the face of these positive trends, several challenges confront HBCUs. While there is some growth in black family income, the problems of high poverty rates among black children remains a serious problem. After falling to a record low poverty rate of 30 percent in 2001, the poverty rate for black children has been increasing to 33.2 percent in 2005 before starting to fall again in 2006 to its current level of 32.6 percent.[16] The persistence of poverty as a southern phenomena continues to be a challenge for HBCUs, most of which are located in the South.[17]

Historically Black Colleges and Universities benefit from a rising college participation rate among black children. However, they face a challenge of declining birth rates for black America. The birth rate for married black women fell from 79.7 live births per 1,000 married black women in 1990 to 64.9 in 2002, significantly below the birth rate for married white non-Hispanic women, which was 84.4 in 2002.[18] The birth rate for black women overall has fallen from 22.4 per 1,000 women ages 15 to 44 in 1990 to 16.2 in 2005.[19] Consequently, black enrollment in elementary schools peaked at 5.6 million in 2003 and has fallen to 5.5 million in 2005.[20]

Another challenge facing HBCUs are low graduation rates.[21] In large part this reflects the lower graduation rates for black students compared to white students;[22] but, is offset somewhat because black students, assuming similar student background, are more likely to graduate from HBCUs than non-HBCUs.[23] This creates several challenges for HBCUs. A key part of the challenge is that failure to graduate can lead to defaults on student loans, as students fail to earn the income needed to repay loans or are discouraged by their experience. At the time of the 1998 reauthorization of the Higher Education Act, about one-third of HBCUs had loan default rates above the legislated threshold to retain access to federal student loan programs.[24] Many HBCUs have increased their graduation and retention rates since 1998, in part, spurred on by needs to reduce loan default rates. Between 1998 and 2006, seven HBCUs posted double digit changes in the percentage of students graduating on time. Still, HBCUs face the challenge that several elite colleges and many flagship state universities have higher graduation rates among their black students than is true for HBCUs.[25]

A persistent challenge facing HBCUs is financial resources. For 2004–2005, no HBCU ranked among the top 120 endowments. The 120th ranked endowment was for Mount Holyoke College, which in 2005 had an endowment valued at almost $450 million.[26] If universities followed rules governing foundations, and spent five percent of their endowments on programs, then a $450 million endowment would add $22.5 million additional funds to the operations of a university. The problems smaller endowments face include getting higher yields on the investment of endowment funds; the rich do get richer—average yields are higher for endowments over $1 billion, and lower for those in the $500 million to $1 billion range.[27] A recent survey of endowment fund performance for fiscal year 2007 showed that endowments earned an average 16.9 percent return.

The many positive trends that HBCUs have to build on make the future look positive for black colleges. HBCUs will have to find a way to successfully recruit the surge in black students with associate degrees to take full advantage of the growth in black college attendance. And, HBCUs will have to find ways to address their challenges of increasing graduation rates and increasing financial resources. HBCUs will have to continue and to build on their leadership in producing black students in engineering and the sciences, a comparative advantage that will be maintained only by raising the bar and expecting even more of the HBCU community.

END NOTES

[1] Xiaojie Li, X. (2007). *Characteristics of Minority-Serving Institutions and Minority Undergraduates Enrolled in These Institutions: Postsecondary Education Descriptive Analysis Report* (NCES 2008-156). National Center for Education Statistics, Institute of Education Sciences, U.S. Department of Education. Table 1-A.
[2] Li, X. (2007). Table 1-B.
[3] Laura G. Knapp, Janice E. Kelly-Reid, Roy W. Whitmore, Shiying Wu, Lorrie Gallego, June Cong, Marcus Berzofsky, Seungho Huh, Burton Levine, and Susan G. Broyles, "Postsecondary Institutions in the United States: Fall 2003 and Degrees and Other Awards Conferred: 2002–03," *Education Statistics Quarterly*, Vol. 7 (Issues 1 & 2), Table 7 [Accessed on the Internet, January 16, 2007: http://nces.ed.gov/programs/quarterly/vol_7/1_2/5_12.asp#1].
[4] Li, X. (2007), Table 2.
[5] Li, X. (2007). Table 3-A.
[6] Li, X. (2007), Table 4-B.
[7] Li, X. (2007). Table 13.
[8] Li, X. (2007). Table 14-A.
[9] Li, X. (2007). Table 14-B.
[10] Li, X. (2007) Table 14-A.
[11] Li, X. (2007) Table 14-B.
[12] Roland G. Fryer and Michael Greenstone, "The Causes and Consequences of Attending Historically Black Colleges and Universities," April 2007, unpublished working paper, 14 [Accessed on January 17, 2007 at: http://www.economics.harvard.edu/faculty/fryer/files/fryer-greenstone%20HBCUs.pdf].
[13] American Council of Education, Minorities in Higher Education Twenty-second Annual Status Report (Washington, DC: ACE, 2006).
[14] See, U.S. Census Bureau Web site, accessed January 17, 2008 at: http://www.census.gov/hhes/www/income/histinc/h01b.html for Black household income, and at: http://www.census.gov/hhes/www/income/histinc/h01w.html for white household income.
[15] See, U.S. Census Bureau Web site, accessed January 17, 2008 at: http://www.census.gov/hhes/www/income/histinc/h03b.html.
[16] See, U.S. Census Bureau Web site, accessed January 17, 2008 at: http://www.census.gov/hhes/www/poverty/histpov/hstpov3.html.
[17] William E. Spriggs, "The Changing Face of Poverty in America," *American Prospect* (May 2007).
[18] Division of Vital Statistics, National Center for Health Statistics, Centers for Disease Control and Prevention. Birth rates for married women, by age, race, and Hispanic origin: United States, 2002.

[19] See Centers for Disease Control, National Center for Health Statistics Web site, accessed January 17, 2008 at: http://www.cdc.gov/nchs/data/nvsr/nvsr56/nvsr56_06.pdf Table 1.

[20] See U.S. Census Bureau Web site: at http://www.census.gov/population/socdemo/school/TableA-1.xls

[21] Florence A. Hamrick, John H. Schuh and Mack C. Shelley, II, "Predicting Higher Education Graduation Rates from Institutional Characteristics and Resource Allocation," *Education Policy Analysis Archives*, 12 (Number 19) Accessed January 17, 2008 from http://epaa.asu.edu/epaa/v12n19/

[22] Yolanda K. Kodryzycki, "College Completion Gaps Between Blacks and Whites: What Accounts for Regional Differences?" *New England Economic Review*, 2004 issue. Accessed January 17, 2008 at: http://www.bos.frb.org/economic/neer/neer2004/neer04b.pdf

[23] Fryer and Greenstone.

[24] Fred J. Galloway and Watson Scott Swail, "Institutional Retention Strategies at Historically Black Colleges and Universities and Their Effects on Cohort Default Rates: 1987–1995," Sallie Mae Education Institute (November 1999).

[25] "Black Student College Graduation Rates Inch Higher But a Large Racial Gap Persists," *Journal of Blacks in Higher Education*, Winter 2007 Preview, accessed January 18, 2008 at: http://www.jbhe.com/preview/winter07preview.html

[26] National Center for Education Statistics Web site, accessed January 18, 2008 at: http://nces.ed.gov/programs/digest/d06/tables/xls/tabn357.xls

[27] Geraldine Fabrikant, "How Smaller College Endowments Still Reap Big Returns," *New York Times*, November 4, 2007.

[28] Erin Strout, "Educational Endowments See 16.9 Percent Return in 2007," *Chronicle of Higher Education*, Friday, January 18, 2008.

Improving Fundraising Efforts at HBCUs

Dr. William R. Harvey
President, Hampton University

While many of our HBCUs are doing well, some of these institutions are experiencing financial difficulties and are struggling to remain open. Implementing new approaches to fundraising may assist in improving their financial viability. Based upon the Hampton Model, this article offers recommendations that can assist in enhancing fundraising strategies.

Introduction

Some of our Historically Black Colleges and Universities (HBCUs) are faced with unprecedented pressure to maintain educational quality, equity and access while coping with shrinking financial bases and declining public confidence. Fletcher (2002), points out how several of our colleges and universities "have been given warnings or placed on probation by accreditation agencies, mostly for financial problems. Still others are struggling with inadequate budgets, antiquated facilities, underprepared students and aging and underfinanced facilities."

It is no secret that several HBCUs are either experiencing financial difficulty or headed for financial trouble. These serious financial difficulties are imposing a growing need for vastly improved fiscal stewardship and better management of all types of college and university resources, thus forcing our colleges and universities to discipline expenditures and implement more effective managerial practices. However, to remain viable and vibrant in the academic landscape and to maintain excellence, colleges and universities must be concerned with strategic planning, positive image building, revenue generation, and skillful resource allocation.

According to Bornstein (2003, p.127), fundraising campaigns "have played a major role in the shaping of American higher education." Bornstein

(2003, p.127) further states that "Throughout the history of American higher education, philanthropy has played a significant role in building facilities, developing academic programs, recruiting students and faculty, and balancing budgets." Because effective fundraising is crucial to the operation of institutions of higher education, HBCUs must make it a priority to improve their fundraising practices.

I will offer some "nuts and bolts" advice as well as share recommendations and observations gleaned from over 30 years of fundraising leadership as a college president. Specifically, I will discuss the president's role in fundraising, the importance of strategic planning, and the development functions as a fundraising strategy. I am pleased to offer this information because these three components have been key to our fundraising success at Hampton University.

The President's Role in Fundraising

Presidential leadership is necessary in setting the climate and in laying a solid foundation for effective fundraising. "The president has the ultimate responsibility for fundraising—for its tone, its priority among other activities, its purposes, and its success. Others play vital roles, such as the trustee leaders and other volunteers, and still others devote more time, such as the vice President for institutional advancement and advancement professionals, but the role of the President is unique. The President is the architect, the enabler, the umpire, the spokesperson, the cheerleader, the persuasive advocate, the tireless champion for the campaign. He or she is the face behind the budgets, the person behind the programs, the voice behind the case statements, and the spirit behind the effort. The President's role in fundraising demands much in terms of time and personal commitment." (Rhodes, 1977, p.11).

The President's leadership role in fundraising is directional and multi-dimensional. For instance, my work demands that I be active in making solicitation calls to corporate and foundation officials; state and federal agency personnel; visiting alumni and friends; interacting with and testifying before congressional committees and various special interest groups. It is also my responsibility to create and sustain an atmosphere of cooperation and teamwork which will enable our development and business officers to be responsible stewards of the resources that we are fortunate enough to secure.

At Hampton University, there is a team management approach used in the fundraising process. Leadership is provided by the President and concerted input is provided by each staff position. The President personifies and communicates the college's goals and character of the college. We have found that successful results in our development efforts have been related to the president's role and ability in exemplifying the character and lifestyles, the hopes and aspirations of all those who comprise Hampton University, i.e., faculty and staff, students, alumni, trustees and friends. Moreover, our experience is that benefactors are becoming more discriminating in their selection of institutions to support. Sophisticated donors want to know what the institution is trying to accomplish and how it expects to achieve its objectives. Therefore, our strategy has been to develop a recognizable image for Hampton—one that is unusually appealing and grounded in a thorough knowledge of the institution. As you know, people give to institutions whose representatives exude clarity, solidarity and confidence with respect to the directions of the college. These characteristics have been incorporated in our marketing strategy.

In my judgment, the president must be primarily responsible for fundraising. How the president accomplishes this mission depends greatly upon his/her personality and style of operation. No matter what other valuable contributions the president makes to the quality of the institution he/she serves, attracting a brilliant faculty and able student body, encouraging academic innovations, and/or ensuring prudent management of the resources of the institution, the president will have failed if he/she does not provide for the institution's financial need.

The Importance of Strategic Planning

It is essential for college presidents to share their vision of the future with prospective donors. After all, people invest in the future; they do not give to the past. In this regard, strategic planning emerges as an indispensable part of any successful fundraising effort. Without strategic planning, there can be little hope for sustained, purposeful action, both within the institution and among its public. Trustees must be educated on the importance of strategic planning, as they should make strategic planning a part of institutional policy.

Secondly, out of strategic planning should come the institution's mission statement, summing up the academic identity of the institution. A good mission statement covers the type of educational institution the university is, the kind of educational philosophy it espouses, and the specific educational aims and purposes it seeks to fulfill.

Institutional needs will emerge from strategic planning. They must be prioritized and translated into fundraising objectives. This list of needs almost certainly will include some things for which fundraising is impractical, some things for which fundraising may be marginally possible, and some for which there is a relatively good shot. The pragmatic task at this point is to establish which of those needs are most palatable and fundable. Some objectives, no matter how desirable, will not bring in gifts. And it does not make sense to spin your wheels in a futile effort to raise money for them.

Thirdly, in my judgment, not enough attention is paid to the institutional case statement, which is a key management tool in successful fund-generating activities. The case statement sets forth the argument for the institution—its educational goal and program, past and present accomplishments, distinctive role in higher education, services to students and community, value to society, future opportunities, requirements for faculty, students, facilities and finances, and plans for accomplishing future goals.

To secure volunteer leadership or funds from whatever source, a psychological sequence must take place before success results. The factors of this sequence are attention, interest, confidence, conviction, desire and action. The best means of telescoping these factors over the shortest possible time span is the case statement. Therefore, the case statement must:

- Serve to justify and explain the institution, its programs and needs so as to lead to advocacy and actual support.
- Attempt to win the reader and evolve from a larger reference of institutional role and societal need to the particular role of your institution.
- Be positive, forward looking and confident with all facts and projections. Be reasonable, clear, vital and accurate.
- Set forth the fundraising plans in terms of policy, priority and enduring results.

Armed with an accurate and well-crafted case statement, college presidents and their fundraising teams can begin to stalk large game, i.e., major gifts. A persistent effort to cultivate and solicit major gift prospects is a critical success factor for surviving and thriving in a competitive environment. The systematic effort to obtain major gifts requires a combined effort involving the board of trustees, the president, the development staff, faculty, other administrators and volunteers.

The President sets the pace in obtaining major gifts by:

- Being willing to take on a number of major gift prospects on his/her own.
- Maintaining continuous cultivation of these prospects, utilizing birthdays, anniversaries, and social events as opportunities for special attention and recognition.

- Involving major gift prospects in the life of the institution – lectures, dramatic events, service on advisory boards, or special committees.
- Ascertaining the special interests of major gift prospects and submitting major proposals that will be of unusual interest and challenge.
- Involving trustees and other influential volunteers with the cultivation and solicitation of these major gifts.

The Development Function as a Fundraising Strategy

While presidents are ultimately responsible for fundraising, they need to find a competent chief development officer with whom they can share their fundraising and public relations programs in an environment of complete confidence. Presidents and development officers should complement each other in administrative skills and working styles. Together, presidents and chief development officers must build and keep a strong development staff.

My work has demanded that I be concerned about the leadership role in the development of people to participate in and to manage Hampton University. My officers and our predecessors have shared this concern, and that is why Hampton University has attained its place in the American educational enterprise as a Class A institution of high quality.

At Hampton University, development is not just another word for fundraising, but is an overall institutional approach to (1) determining the role the college should play in higher education; (2) projecting a program to realize the institution's highest destiny; and (3) bringing the full strength of the college and its publics to bear on achieving the goals necessary to implement this program.

Therefore, the development function is clearly defined administratively with a well-articulated plan for strengthening the educational program of the college—a plan that indicates the profile of the students and faculty members desired, the size of the enrollment ultimately planned, the curriculum envisioned, and the physical facilities required.

I find that at least three conditions must be present to guarantee a successful development program:

- **There must be a thoroughly prepared and well-documented academic blueprint. This is to be a plan that shows where the institution has been, where it is now, and where it proposes to go in carrying out its program of service to society.** The plan should stress why society needs the institution rather than the needs of the institution itself. The plan has to include a long-term financial projection as well as a method of obtaining the income to reach these objectives.

- **A sound development program has an "inner core" of persons who believe in the institution and its program and who are willing to use every ounce of their energies to make the program a success.** The most important person in the core is the president. Next in importance are the vice president in charge of development and his/her staff members. The chairman of the board of trustees and members of the board of trustees who are willing to place top priority on development activities are important to the development process.

- **There must be a timetable of action to turn the institutional goals into accomplished realities.** The program of action should contain short-term goals that can be attained within an academic year as well as long-term goals. The action program includes the building of an organization of many volunteers, each of whom will be assigned a specific task in accordance with his or her ability of interest. The program has to include a study of prospective donors who will be approached to help underwrite educational projects of particular interest to them.

Management of a development program is obviously important. Many factors influence the success of a development program – factors such as well-defined aims, long-range planning, a strong board of trustees, and interested volunteers. However, one of the major reasons for success in development is effective management of the development program itself. This is the direct responsibility of the chief development officer, a major responsibility of the president, and a matter of concern and interest of the development committee of the board of trustees.

I will now present some guidelines that I use in the leadership of our development program:

- Measure success by (1) adequate funds for current operations and capital growth, (2) understanding and acceptance of the institution's program, and (3) students of the kind and quantity the institution needs. Everything the staff members do should help to realize one of these objectives.

- Set specific goals for the entire department and each area within the department. These goals should include the amount of money to be raised during the year, dollar objectives for each staff member, the number of donors and prospects to be contacted, and the number of calls to be made by each staff member on a monthly basis.

- The development staff should be organized to give effective support to the fundraising effort. Among other things, this means making a minimum number of calls every week and month. Clearly, the calls must be made on the right prospects, and obviously the staff should provide research, background information and fundraising strategies, including help from volunteers to make these calls effective.

- The development staff must stress teamwork. Real teamwork is based on each staff member's knowing the major issues confronting the department and the institution and how his own task fits into the big picture. This requires regular meetings of the entire development and advancement staff. At Hampton, in addition to the weekly internal meetings within the development division, the development leadership meets once per week with the president.

- The major emphasis must be placed on major gifts. I always stress to my staff that quality time must be spent where the greatest gift potential lies. There should be a list of major gift prospects for each constituent group.

We find that good management in a development program demands effective coordination and the use of communications and public relations tools—publications, special events, publicity, personal appearances, etc. The public relations staff functions as cooperating members of the development team, never losing sight of the chief task of obtaining understanding and support for the college. A degree of caution about public relations should be noted here. Studies have shown that private institutions that allocate the larger part of their development budget to public relations and publications tend to be low in gifts. Those colleges that allocate the larger part of their development budget to fundraising tend to be high in gifts. You may want to examine your own programs to determine where your budgetary emphasis is and whether your gifts fall in the high or low category.

Institutional advancement, development, and fundraising are often used interchangeably to mean those activities designed to bring to an institution acceptance and support from each of its constituent groups. To be successful in this most important activity requires that we have a unified program within our respective institutions that is coordinated by the chief executive. At Hampton, that process involves every administrative officer, although in varying degrees of activity.

Conclusion

Considering the severe financial problems that some HBCUs face, there is a need to improve fundraising efforts and strategies. The president of an HBCU or any institution of higher education plays a very important role in successful fundraising. Strategic planning, a clear and compelling mission and case statement, along with having an effective development program are necessary to steer one's institutional ship through turbulent but navigable waters. The Hampton model has proven to be enormously successful. I recommend it to you for your consideration in improving fundraising efforts at your institution.

REFERENCES

Bornsteirn, R. (2003). *Legitimacy in the Academic Presidency From Entrance to Exit. American.* Westport, CT: American Council on Education and Praeger Publishers.

Fletcher, M. (2002). At Black Colleges, Disparate Fortunes. *Washington Post.* Retrieved from http:llwww.washingtonpost.com/ac2/wp-dyn/A28060-2002Nov22?language=printer.

Rhodes, F. (1997). *Successful Fundraising for Higher Education The Advancing of Learning.* Phoenix, Arizona: The American Council on Education and The Oryx Press.

The State of America's Black Colleges

Dr. Trudie Kibbe Reed
President, Bethune-Cookman University

Introduction

As a baby boomer who endured segregation and a segregated educational system all the way through high school, I understand and embrace the value of *living and learning* within a traditional African-American context. As I reflect back on my youth and the integration movement, there are few remaining relics or symbols of hope today that transmit our culture, traditions, and heritage. Essentially, the core values of our once endowed community of hope have given way to a broken covenant that has fostered despair, confusion, and general hopelessness among our youth.

There are few remnants of the proud and accomplished African-American communities except for the black church, Greek organizations, historic advocacy organizations such as the NAACP and Urban League, and of course our beloved Historically Black Colleges and Universities (HBCUs). These institutions are entrusted to guide our youth through the journey into a global society that currently gives little definition to the struggles and reconciliation of an oppressed race of people. We must never allow these institutions to die or become diluted because they are instrumental in fostering academic achievement, strong values, and character in all aspects of the community.

The article will highlight the importance of institutional effectiveness processes in strengthening and continuing the rich legacy of our HBCUs.

Environmental Forecasting

Many minority students have obstacles they must overcome to obtain an education and advance economically. This is certainly not a new dilemma, and building on the transformative vision of racial equality propagated fifty years earlier in *Brown v. Board of Education,* the Supreme Court insisted in 2003 that eliminating the opportunity fissures for African Americans and other minorities is an American imperative: "Effective participation by members of all racial and ethnic groups in the civic life of our Nation is essential if the dream of one Nation, indivisible, is to be realized" *(Grutter v. Bollinger, 2003)*. Environmental scanning and monitoring are important contributions for examining the external environment and predicting student success. Over the years, a national consensus of business leaders, educators, and legislatures have concluded that the black-white achievement gap is of critical concern for our country and must be addressed. Yet, many African-American students continue to attend segregated, high-poverty elementary and secondary schools (Orfield and Yun, 1999) that tend to have less-qualified teaching staff, deteriorating facilities, fewer up-to-date textbooks, lower average test scores, and fewer advanced placement courses *(Grutter v.Bollinger, 2003)*. In addition, African-American students are overrepresented in special education classes and low-track placements but underrepresented in gifted and talented programs (Losen and Orfield, 2002). Fifty years after *Brown*, we still have not attained what was mandated by the judicial system.

As the gap between African Americans and whites in their wages, employment, and residence expands, HBCUs are narrowing the gap between the races. Their students are globally competitive and capable of making positive contributions to the economy and society (Garces, Thomas, and Currie; 2002). The depth and breadth of this gap, at least with respect to educational achievement, may be best expressed by the statistics. If you are an African American 25 years of age or older, you are more likely to be *without* a high school diploma than you are to *have* a college degree. Conversely, if you are white and in the same age group, you are nearly *three* times as likely to have a college degree than you are to be without a high school diploma (U.S. Census March 2002).

Although it is true that minorities can apply to any institution of higher learning now, applying is different from being admitted. Admittance does not guarantee that students are included and accepted into the campus culture. At a time when test scores often determine admission, there is no question that many minorities will fall short in this area. Most minority students lack the financial resources to pay for extensive test preparation courses. However, many HBCUs admit students that would be turned away at traditional institutions. Many of these students have skills that cannot be measured on a paper and pencil test. Since the mid-1800s, HBCUs have provided superb education and training to many Americans. These schools opened the door to African Americans when other doors were shamefully closed. Since their inception, these schools have furthered the development of young people, who have gone on to become leaders in government, business, education, science, the military, law, and many other fields.

Strategic Planning for Institutional Effectiveness

Most HBCUs' missions are like Bethune-Cookman's: they seek to serve the cultural needs of their students—traditional and nontraditional—and to develop the desire and capacity for continuous intellectual and professional growth, leadership and service to others. Both HBCU and majority institutions have to plan strategically to meet objectives and/or goals and are evaluated on their institutional effectiveness.

Many HBCUs are struggling because we have devalued the importance of environmental scanning, strategic planning, and assessment leading to quality control, accountability, and corrective actions prior to crisis intervention and/or catastrophic circumstances.

Financial stability comes from effective strategic planning that allows an institution to be proactive in finding solutions as soon as problems are identified. Many institutions view institutional effectiveness as time consuming and complicated. In fact, institutional effectiveness processes are the only way to continue legacies and develop alternative pathways to eliminate deficits, chronic low enrollment, and ineffective performance of those who lead or manage institutions of higher learning.

The process of evaluating institutional effectiveness allows an institution to demonstrate how well it succeeds in accomplishing its mission and meeting its goals. The process allows each university to choose its expected outcomes based on its *self-identified mission*. Therefore, a well-defined mission is essential. The faculty and administrators develop mission statements for each academic program and administrative unit that are derived from the university mission statement. Then, they define the program and learning outcomes they believe are most appropriate and report these in an annual assessment cycle. The outcomes help determine the extent to which the institution achieved its mission in that planning year. Finally, the assessment results are used as the basis for making changes for continuous improvements in the academic and administrative programs. These results also play a large role in forecasting success at the state and federal levels.

Achievement of institutional effectiveness is equal to the institutions' commitment to teaching, research, community service and assisting students in building personal values. HBCUs are highly effective in this manner. HBCUs award 25 percent of African-American baccalaureate degrees even though they represent just 3 percent of the nation's more than 4,000 colleges and universities, which speaks volumes of their success. HBCUs administer more than 400 programs, including scholarship, internship and fellowship programs, mentoring, summer enrichment, and curriculum and faculty development programs.

For the first time in 2007, the *U.S. News and World Report* magazine ranked both private and state-funded HBCUs. Though many have concerns regarding the methodology and weighted criteria of the report, the rankings of black colleges in itself is a tribute to what they have been able to accomplish in comparison to their larger counterparts. Many of these institutions, especially the private institutions have had to overcome extraordinary financial challenges. It is worth noting that two colleges, Xavier University, ranked eighth by *U.S. News and World Report* magazine, and Dillard University, ranked ninth, are located in New Orleans and were forced to close temporarily by Hurricane Katrina in 2005. Future rankings suggest a shift from obscure comparisons to the highlighting of mission similarities of HBCUs while emphasizing their programmatic strengths and the impact these institutions have on society.

Assessment of Quality: The State of HBCUs (A Job Well Done)

In reviewing program quality, one does not have to look far for praise. HBCUs have been lauded by a list of state legislatures as well as President Bush for their "high standards of excellence, for preparing rising generations for success and for helping to fulfill the nation's commitment to quality equal education" (September 9, 2005 Press Release).

HBCUs have enabled thousands of African Americans to achieve higher education and to compete in the global economy. Since the 1960s, a number of studies have been conducted to determine the quality of HBCU programs. Most recent studies suggest no statistical difference between the educational experiences of students attending HBCUs for undergraduate education; however, one significant difference between HBCUs and majority institutions is the retention rate of African Americans. When comparing similar programs, 66 percent of all African Americans who graduated from traditionally white institutions received a degree or remained in the program in comparison with 82 percent of students who graduated from HBCUs (ETS, 2004). These studies speak to the quality programs at HBCUs and their ability to do more with less.

In Arkansas, the statistics continue to confirm a job well done. Forty percent of all African Americans receiving bachelor's degrees in the state of Arkansas graduated from HBCUs. Last year, 100 percent of the African-American graduates from the University of Arkansas Medical School were HBCU graduates. Many HBCU graduates testify that despite coming from poor educational backgrounds, HBCU faculty from similar backgrounds nurtured them and helped them to graduate.

According to the United Negro College Fund:

- Over half of all African-American professionals are graduates of HBCUs.
- Nine of the top ten colleges that graduate the most African Americans who go on to earn Ph.D.s are HBCUs.
- More than 50 percent of the nation's African-American public school teachers and 70 percent of African-American dentists earned degrees at HBCUs.
- UNCF members Spelman College and Bennett College produce over half of the nation's African-American female doctorates in all science fields.
- As ranked by *Black Enterprise* in 2003, seven of the top ten "Top Colleges and Universities for African Americans," including the top six, were HBCUs.
- HBCU Xavier University is number one nationally in placing African Americans into medical school.
- The first *Time Magazine/Princeton Review* HBCU "College of the Year" is, Florida A&M University. It is the number one producer of African Americans with baccalaureate degrees.
- Tuskegee University is the only college ever to be designated a national historic site by the U.S. Congress.

Strengthening HBCUs Through Environmental Forecasting

"The key to strengthening HBCUs is in the continued performance of its students and alumni. HBCUs must continue to expend their influence upon the lives of African Americans and other ethnic minorities as well as economically marginalized white Americans," said Ernest L. Holloway, President Emeritus of Langston University (2001 Press Release). In 2007, many question the role or the need for HBCUs. Prior to desegregation, it was clear that HBCUs had an obligation to educate minorities. However, today, when African Americans are not barred from majority institutions, have HBCUs outlived their purpose?

Only those with a narrow view of society and little knowledge of the issues in our urban communities will have difficulty answering the above question. HBCUs, like African Americans as a whole, must reclaim their own community rights. They must review and reevaluate our traditional mission and strategic focus to meet contemporary needs of the black society. Even under close scrutiny, the state of HBCUs is strong. However, to confront the challenges facing today's youth, HBCUs must use strategic planning to secure the future. Although in recent years, individual HBCUs may have experienced problems, as a whole, our institutions continue to flourish. Even when educating students that other institutions turn away, HBCUs must navigate the winds to keep their tuitions affordable and programs of high quality.

America must admit that there are stark disparities between the education that black and white students receive in public schools. America must recognize that there is a gap in student achievement and that HBCUs will continue to fill this gap with determined focus. In essence, "it takes a village." HBCU stakeholders must unite to do this important work. Even under the watchful eye of a perhaps overcritical society, the courts have become increasingly concerned that HBCUs promote separate and unequal structures of higher education. The local, state, and federal governments have to share in the vision of the differences made today and what from these HBCUs will be most useful tomorrow.

HBCUs must strive to not only meet the expectations of the 1992 Supreme Court case *(U.S. v Fordice)* but also to exceed the judicial mandates that have forced many HBCUs to expand their missions. Researchers have distinguished a variety of areas in which HBCUs have excelled over traditionally white institutions in the education of black students, but the debate will not end there. HBCUs must use both the quantitative and qualitative data collected each year to improve performance of students, faculty, staff, administrators, programs and services as the information suggests. Each HBCU must continue to review the areas of excellence as well as the areas for improvement to retool and best advocate for minority students. Alumni must also do their job by giving back to the institutions from which they have gained so much.

Graduates of historically black colleges and universities have made great contributions to America and continue to serve as role models for all Americans. The struggles and many successes of America's historically black colleges and universities are the struggles and successes of our nation. HBCUs are committed to excellence and play an integral role within our higher education system. As recent Bethune-Cookman University graduate Nicole Brown stated, "My undergraduate experience was phenomenal; it taught me the importance of tradition. In the same light, it brought on a fascination for change and exposed the benefits of continuing on with higher education. The words of caring professors along with some other experiences have helped me realize that educating myself is the only way that my voice could be heard. If I do not educate myself, my past experiences will surmount my future endeavors."

Our nation must continue to support HBCUs for the sake of our students and our future. African Americans have to become more self-reliant in their expectations of the work in keeping HBCUs relevant in the twenty-first century. If African-Americans support, help restructure, and take responsibility for their institutions, then HBCUs will gain new respect and a broader audience for the successes they strive to continue.

REFERENCES

Daniel J. Losen and Gary Orfield, "Introduction," in *Racial Inequity in Special Education*, eds. Daniel J. Losen and Gary Orfield (Cambridge, MA: Civil Rights Project, Harvard Education Press, 2002), xvi–xvii.

Douglas S. Massey, "Residential Segregation and Neighborhood Conditions in U.S. Metropolitan Areas," in *America Becoming*, Vol. 1, eds. Neil J. Smelser et al. (National Research Council, 2001), 399, 401.

Eliana Garces, Duncan Thomas, and Janet Currie, "Longer-Term Effects of Head Start," *The American Economic Review*, Vol. 92, No. 4. (Sept., 2002), pp. 999–1012.

ETS. "Students at Historically Black Colleges and Universities: Their Aspirations and Accomplishments." 2004. ETS Mar 2004. http://www.ets.org/research/pic/hbcprefa.html.

Gary Orfield and John Yun, *Resegregation in American Schools* (Cambridge, MA: Civil Rights Project, 1999).

Grutter vs. Bollinger, Certiorari to the United States Court of Appeals for the Sixth Circuit No.02-241 argued April 1, 2003–decided June 23, 2003.

Janny Scott, "Rethinking Segregation Beyond Black and White," New York *Times*, July 29, 2001.

Press Release: Committee on Education and the Workforce, Chairman John Boehner (April 24, 2001).

Sandra Ruppert, *Closing the College Participation Gap: A National Summary* (Center for Community College Policy, October 2003).

Segregation Matters: Poverty and Educational Inequality (Cambridge, MA: Civil Rights Project, 2005), 6–7.

U.S. Census Bureau, Educational Attainment of the Population 25 Years Over by Sex, and Race and Hispanic Origin: March 2002, http://www.census.gov/population/socdemo/race/black/ppl-164/tab07.pdf.

A Cause Worth Joining:
Educating African-American Males at ASU

Dr. Everette J. Freeman
President, Albany State University

The Early Years

Long before the plight of African-American males received national notoriety, Albany State University (ASU) in Albany, Georgia, recognized the rapidly decreasing presence of African-American males in college and responded by creating a sweeping scholarly research and action initiative by establishing the Center for the Study of the Black Male.

Created in 1988 by then-President Dr. Billy C. Black, the Center for the Study of the Black Male was developed to address the glaring need for research about the state of the African-American male at a time when national statistics painted a contrasting picture of both success and failure. The media portrayed a dual image of the African-American male as leading among athletes and entertainers, as well as the nation's homicide victims, high school drop-outs, and prisoners.

In 1988, the problems affecting African-American males spanned the spectrum. In elementary and secondary education, their suspension and drop-out rates were the highest among any ethnic group. In the criminal justice system, their incarceration rate outnumbered college enrollment. In the workplace, African-American male achievers in business lagged significantly behind their white counterparts and endured a far higher rate of unemployment.

Of these issues impacting the African-American male and, ultimately, the African-American family, two things were certain:

1. Just as Historically Black Colleges and Universities (HBCUs) played a unique role in addressing the once-glaring disparity in access to higher education for African Americans, HBCUs must develop programs to address the specific needs of the African-American male.

2. Failure to reduce the widening education gap between African-American males and other groups would produce disastrous consequences for all of America.

Albany State University's leadership quickly determined that reversing low college enrollment among African-American males was a critical issue, one requiring widespread support, strategic planning and focused programming rooted in early intervention.

The Center hosted its first planning conference in 1989, partnering with the Southeast Region of the NAACP, and established satellite programs at Fort Valley State University and Savannah State University later that year. Increasing support among key stakeholders was the primary focus of the Center's early years as President Black and the Center's first director, Dr. Nelson Onyenwoke, sought an answer for the looming crisis.

An Expanded Focus: From Research to Action

Challenges of the 1990s would require the Center to expand its focus from one of research to action. National enrollment and graduation statistics revealed the following:

- African-American males represented less than one-third of the growth in the total proportion of African-American undergraduate students in degree-granting institutions nationwide between 1990 and 2004.

- Less than half (43 percent) of all African-American students who enrolled in a four-year college as first-time freshmen in 1995–1996 had completed a bachelor's degree by 2001, compared to 63 percent of white students and an alarming 36 percent for black males.

The statistics provided a snapshot of African-American male students at the beginning and end of the college education process; however, they failed to address the specific dynamics impacting the enrollment, retention and graduation rates of African-American males. Individual characteristics—such as family background, academic preparation, and socio-economic status—often influence the decision to attend college and complete a degree, with academic preparation and family background as the strongest of the three.

A study of African-American performance on standardized tests as compared to the performance of students in other ethnic groups identified elementary school as the start of the achievement gap for African-American students, specifically African-American males. For these children, a range of challenges were connected to the disparity in achievement, including higher poverty levels, lower levels of education among parents, family and school instability, inexperienced teachers, and peer pressure.

The problems plaguing the African-American male were clear, and Albany State University was among the first in Georgia to turn its attention to developing solutions. The Center for the Study of the Black Male, later named the Center for the African-American Male (CAAM), soon implemented a comprehensive program designed to address the needs of "at-risk" male students.

CAAM: Southwest Georgia's Agent for Change

Albany State University's CAAM aims to do one thing— improve the lives of African-American males in Southwest Georgia by increasing college enrollment and graduation rates. CAAM seeks to achieve this goal through a variety of programs focused on recruitment, retention, and mentoring.

Early studies identified several barriers to the recruitment of male students in higher education, ranging from poor grades to financial concerns. Today, CAAM seeks to remove many of the perceived barriers to college enrollment for African-American males. CAAM students work with young men of all ages to increase their access and exposure to Albany State University by connecting with more than 1,300 students from surrounding public schools each year. Each month, CAAM invites a neighboring school to visit ASU for campus tours and college preparation workshops as a part of the "Day on the Yard" with CAAM initiative.

Retention scholars agree that student involvement is a critical component of retention. For African-American men, however, involvement is often adversely affected by challenges that surface during the college transition. CAAM's programming was designed to help ease the transition to college with retention as its primary focus. In 1994, the Saturday Academy was established as a required activity for all CAAM students. In the Academy, guest lecturers discuss a variety of topics essential to the overall growth of our students, such as leadership skills, financial planning, mentoring techniques, and health and wellness. In addition to lectures, students also receive academic advising, counseling, and tutoring. Initially, students joined the center on a volunteer basis. Today, all African-American male students are enrolled in the center upon admission to the University.

Mentoring programs serve a dual purpose for ASU's CAAM students. The Center identifies positive role models to serve as mentors for its students, and the students themselves serve as mentors for young men in the neighboring public school systems. Consequently, both the ASU male students and the younger male students are exposed to positive examples of African-American men and the opportunities afforded by higher education. Last year alone CAAM students mentored 195 fifth-graders in the Dougherty County School System. Approximately 90 percent of those students were promoted to the sixth grade.

The University System of Georgia Responds

In 2000, the University System of Georgia (USG) turned its attention to the low percentage of African-American males enrolled in the university system in comparison to the percentage of African-American males in the population. For example, within the USG, African-American females outnumbered African-American males two to one (28,000 to 14,000) even though the percentage of African-American males and females in the population was about the same.

In response, in 2001 the USG developed a special funding initiative to identify barriers to the participation of African-American males in the university system and the following institutions and programs were awarded $10,000 each in African-American Male Initiative (AAMI) pilot initiative funding:

- **Albany State University:** To support the institution's summer bridge programs for African-American students and to foster information sharing regarding their success in achieving the third-highest retention rate in the university System.

- **Atlanta Metropolitan College:** To support the college's long-running Saturday Academy/PREP initiative, which identifies and cultivates underprepared students in the K–12 pipeline and enhances their preparation for college admissions and matriculation.

- **Coastal Georgia Community College:** To support President Dorothy Lord's 10-year-old Coastal Georgia Minority Out-reach Program, a community-college partnership that targets dozens of rising seventh-grade African-American males living in Brunswick and along the southeast Georgia coast for mentoring and tutoring activities aimed at enhancing their college preparation and reducing the rate of high-school dropouts.

- **Fort Valley State University:** To support the launch of FVSU's three-week, pre-collegiate summer residential institute for a small sample of underprepared (limited admissions) students, focusing on reading, writing, mathematics, study skills, time management, library skills, and other areas in which they need additional preparation.

- **Savannah State University:** To provide funding for the institution's successful PREP and TRIO programs and to help launch their new Summer Pipeline Program, aimed at developing underprepared students for college matriculation. Special efforts focused on the transition of African-American male students from these pre-college programs into the university and on enhancing the institution's recent increases in the SAT scores of first-time freshmen.

- **The University of Georgia:** To support Dr. Deryl Bailey's "Project: Gentle-men on the Move," a mentoring and academic-support program that has been implemented successfully in three states. The program aims to increase the number of college prep and advanced college courses successfully completed by program participants, thereby equipping them with the academic and social skills they will need to be successful in institutions of higher learning.

In July 2002, there were three known programs in the USG focusing on improving black males' educational participation. Today there are more than 20 such programs at 15 different USG institutions focusing on the K–12 pipeline, college retention, leadership development and student life.

The Need for Continued Support

Not much has changed on the national front since Dr. Billy Black first tackled the problems concerning the "endangered species" known as the African-American male. In 2008, homicide remains the leading cause of death, and incarceration rates continue to outpace college enrollment. Even more problematic may be the increasing demand for intellectual competence as a prerequisite for college enrollment while African-American students continue to lag in academic achievement.

However, the impact of Dr. Black's work is more than evident in the successes of Albany State University's and the University System of Georgia's African-American male initiatives.

- From fall semester 2006 to fall semester 2007, ASU's CAAM achieved an 80.5 percent retention rate of the first-year students involved with the program.

- Since CAAM's inception, the graduation rate for African-American males at ASU has nearly doubled.
- African-American male enrollment in the University System of Georgia has increased by 24.5 percent—from 17,068 in fall 2002 to 21,249 students in fall 2007.
- Most recent numbers for fall 2007 are up 7.4 percent over year, adding another 1,465 African-American males to the ranks of students at state institutions of higher education.

The success of both initiatives affirms the need for a national commitment to increasing college enrollment and graduation rates of African-American males. For 20 years, Albany State University's has been dedicated to researching and addressing the developmental needs of African-American male collegiate students and youth in Southwest Georgia. I urge you to join the cause.

Learning How, Not What, To Think:
American Women and Liberal Arts Education

Dr. Julianne Malveaux
President, Bennett College for Women

Bennett College for Women is a small, dynamic liberal arts HBCU located in Greensboro, North Carolina. Founded as a co-educational institution in the basement of St. Matthew's Church, the college became an institution for women in 1926. Once known as the "Vassar of the South," Bennett's students and alumnae have been since its founding innovators, leaders, and cutting-edge civil rights activists. The first woman president of Bennett College, Dr. Willa B. Player, opened Annie Pfeiffer Chapel to Dr. Martin Luther King, Jr. in 1958 when no other venue in Greensboro was available to him. Bennett women played a pivotal role in the integration of the Woolworth's lunch counters in 1961; many of them were jailed because of their protest. More recently, 50 Bennett women, led by Student Government Association President Tiffany Lindsey ('08), joined the Jena 6 protest in Jena, Louisiana in September 2007. While other college contingents may have been larger, Bennett's students who traveled to Jena represented 7.5 percent of Bennett College's student body.

Bennett College's liberal arts education features critical thinking, research and writing skills. Students are not taught what to think, but how to think and how to tackle challenges and solve problems. Cognizant of the cost of higher education and the need for developing measurements that calibrate success, colleges track ways to encourage students in their professional development. We look at the number of internships our students receive, the number of students who continue on with graduate education, and job placement. At the same time, these measurable outcomes cannot be the sole goal of higher education. The engagement in the academic enterprise, the encouragement of a love for learning, the development of critical thinking skills, and the promotion of civic engagement are all part of the essential education offered at Bennett College for Women.

In addition, the small, liberal arts, mostly residential campus offers students the opportunity to grow and develop in the context of community.

At our small campus, faculty and staff are closely involved in student life and student development. With 50 student organizations, campus life is abuzz with activities, speakers, films, and gatherings. This rich campus life offers the opportunity for civic engagement, leadership development, and the development of academic acumen.

Bennett College for Women is, of course, not the only HBCU that focuses on a liberal education. With the pace of change so accelerated in the 21st century, it is critical that African-American students, and especially African-American women, consider a liberal education as opposed to "career" education. After all, many contemporary professional workers are holding down jobs in careers that had not even been conceived when they graduated from college. Technology has transformed many careers, and spawned new ones, and it is likely that this transformation will continue in the future. Thus, it is not the specifics of career preparation, but the basics of communication and knowledge transmission, that will determine success or failure for 21st century workers.

As Bennett College for Women moves from good to great, an emerging aspect of our educational offerings is a global experience for students. In the spring of 2008, Cheryl McQueen, a visiting lecturer made available to us through the White House HBCU Initiative and the Department of Commerce, is offering lectures on China—a critical knowledge area given the emergence of China as a key world power. The 2008 Olympics to be held in Beijing signal China's emergence on the world stage. The rapid improvement in China's standard of living has implications for the rest of the worlds as China's energy use will put pressure on oil prices, which have already exceeded $100 a barrel in late 2007 and early 2008. China's intent to diversify its currency holdings, substituting the euro for the dollar for at least part of its portfolio, also has an impact on the United States. To be sure, some observers have overstated the pace of China's transformation, ignoring the fact that more than 300 million Chinese workers earn about a dollar a day. Still, with one in four consumers coming from China, this nation is a factor in our global future. Awareness of China and its role in the global marketplace is an essential part of a liberal arts education, and about a dozen Bennett juniors and seniors, with majors including business, journalism and media studies, and education, will benefit from Professor McQueen's knowledge.

A global initiative cannot focus solely on one country, even one as important as China. Through participation in Mellon Foundation-financed Salzburg seminars, and through the leadership of dedicated faculty, the college's Global Studies Initiative is developing and expanding into one that has a goal of developing a general education course on global understanding and offering every student a global studies experience. The global pace of change is such that countries now seen as small or insignificant may gain significance as world affairs shift. The purpose of studying China is to develop a set of analytical and problem-solving skills that are applicable to a broad set of issues and challenges around global affairs. Similarly, international study and travel experiences expose students to cultural diversity. It also provides them an opportunity to analyze the role of the United States in a global context, and reinforces the importance of developing a broad worldview for 21st century leaders.

Another emerging aspect of a Bennett education is the school's focus on entrepreneurial development. As the core labor market bifurcates into a landscape where some hold "good jobs" with pensions, health care benefits, and sick leave while others hold marginal jobs with scant attention from policy makers, entrepreneurship is key to 21st century educational development. Whether a Bennett student intends to run a business, or work for someone else, the development of a skill that allows her to promote and showcase her talents and abilities is critical.

Entrepreneurial skills are especially critical in the African-American community, as the labor market continues to treat African-Americans and others unevenly. In December 2007, the unemployment rate was five percent, which translated into nine percent for African Americans. Consistently, the African-American unemployment rate has been twice the rate of whites, suggesting that a weak labor market for some is catastrophic for others. One million more African-American women than men work, partly because of structural biases against African-American men in labor markets. A focus on entrepreneurship for African-American women is critical to individual and community survival.

Bennett College for Women is a unique space, yet it shares the mission of providing liberal education for African-American women with several other institutions. Our sister school, Spelman College, is the only other HBCU that focuses on women. Further, in the HBCU landscape there are several small, liberal arts colleges that engage men and women, but mostly women, in the endeavor of gaining a general education that is the foundation for career and lifelong living and learning. Combining unique programs, global foci, and corporate partnership, several other HBCUs exist to provide education to African-American women.

The need for a focus on African-American women is more important now than ever. While nearly one in five African-American women over 25 hold a college degree, up from a scant 1.4 percent in 1940 (Digest of Educational Statistics, 2005), the uneven engagement of African-American women in the labor market and in corporate America is evident. African-American women, though more fully deployed in the labor market than African-American men

(Bureau of Labor Statistics, 2008), are paid less, at the same level of income and education, than white men, white women, and African-American men. African-American women shoulder a significant share of the economic burden in the African-American community, as the sole support of nearly half of all African-American households, and the support of more than half of African-American children. Despite these gaps, it is clear that those African-American women who attain an education are unlikely to earn low wages. Indeed, education is one way to prevent the poverty that plagues one in four African-American households.

Thus, it is important to center on the many ways that HBCUs can empower African-American women. We are the front line in education for first generation college students, those whose parents are often less equipped to negotiate the complexities of higher education enrollment. At Bennett, for example, more than 40 percent of our students are first-generation college students who come with no less intellectual acumen than their sisters whose parents have attended college. Nonetheless, these first-generation students often need assistance in managing the financial complexities of matriculation. The history of African-American matriculation is such that the average African-American student graduates with $26,000 in student loan indebtedness. (The comparable number is $20,000 overall). HBCU graduates have an average of $28,000 in student loan debt.

Does it make sense for students to encumber themselves with this crushing debt? Data suggest that those who attain college degrees will earn more in a lifetime—up to one million dollars more – than those who do not matriculate. However, it is also clear that those who take the most complete advantage of their higher education experience are those who are most likely to see augmented earnings. In other words, those who are engaged campus citizens are more likely to excel in life than those who are not; those who attain the highest academic honors are more likely to enjoy returns to education than those who do not; those who are nurtured, enabled and encouraged are more likely to tackle life's hurdles with enthusiasm than those who have not enjoyed that degree of nurturing.

It is from this perspective that it is possible to make a strong case for matriculation at HBCUs, especially those that serve women. Those students who are able to experience and participate in leadership opportunities at women's colleges are more likely to attain leadership positions after college. There is a disproportionate number of women who serve in corporate, political and civil leadership roles who have graduated from women's colleges. While some would suggest that matriculation at women's colleges is a retreat from the "real world" of diverse interactions and involvement, there are others who would suggest that the women who have the privilege of attending women's colleges are able to develop a unique and effective brand of leadership that may be pivotal in our nation's 21st century development.

As the United States sees its influence wane in the face of a multifaceted global development, the cultivation of thinkers, contributors and leaders who see the world multiculturally is critical. While technology will proliferate at a rapid pace, and knowledge management becomes a new area of skill development, the focus is likely to be on how, not what, we think. As other countries invest more heavily in education than the United States—China, India, and Eastern Europe now produce more engineers than we do—aspects of diverse education become important for this country. Colleges like Bennett, with a strong expertise in the STEM (science, technology, engineering and mathematics) areas, with an emphasis on strong communications and critical thinking, are likely to be the colleges that produce leaders for the future.

Why do these colleges have such an edge? The small student-faculty ratio (about 12-1 at Bennett) means that students are both taught and coached about their academics, career goals, and possibilities for contribution. When campus programs have a co-curricular focus, the institution's priorities are frequently reinforced. With a large number of student activities, students have an opportunity to participate in, and of course observe, diverse models of women's leadership. These are environments where students can absolutely thrive as they grow and develop.

As students thrive, so must these institutions. To be sure, while HBCUs do "heavy lifting" in producing college graduates (we are three percent of the degree granting institutions, and we produce more than 15 percent of the B.A. degree recipients at last count). We now enroll a minority of the African-American students seeking college degrees. These statistics suggest that we produce more efficiently than others because there is something about the quality of education we offer that gives unique support to African-American students.

Similarly, while Bennett College for Women and Spelman College enroll a minority of the African-American women who attend college, those students who complete their education at these unique institutions bring a special set of experiences to the workplace and the world place because of the ways their abilities and confidences were buttressed at these single-sex educational institutions. HBCUs now enroll a minority of African-American students who seek college degrees. What does it take for small, liberal arts HBCUs to improve the ways we deliver education? Many, including Bennett College for Women, are fiscally fragile, with small endowments; physical plants that could stand improvement, and dedicated faculties that need more opportunities for development. From a policy perspective, the special work that we do requires special recognition and assistance. The opportunity to borrow on favorable terms, with low-cost loans, is important. Also, the opportunity for favorable ways to compete with large colleges for federal grants for education and pilot programs helps with our bottom line. Grants to enhance curricula make it possible for our fiscally challenged colleges to provide critical educational offerings.

While many students seek higher education opportunities because they want jobs after graduation, higher education also offers a way to explore opportunities, possibilities and pathways to critical thinking and problem solving. As our nation's demography shifts and African-American women become more pivotal players in the labor market and in the civic arena, it is important to develop this population in its many manifestations. The nurturance of HBCUs like Bennett College is an investment in the survival of thousands of young women, but also in the survival of our nation and our world. The women who are nurtured as critical thinkers at Bennett are women who will contribute to the future of our world because they have been taught how, not what, to think.

Education and Industry Partnerships for Rebuilding New Orleans

Dr. Wayne Watson
Chancellor, City Colleges of Chicago

The lesson learned from Hurricanes Katrina and Rita is less about nature's power to destroy than it is about America's failure to apply its power to address the economic disparities afflicted on African Americans, Hispanics, and poor whites who lived in the Crescent City. New Orleans is now poised to rebuild. Who will participate in—and benefit from—the rebuilding process? Will those who were forced out of their homes have a stake in the rebuilding of their communities and benefit from the economic development opportunities presented by the estimated $200 billion in reconstruction costs for the Gulf Coast region affected by Katrina?[1] Will reconstruction efforts take advantage of this fortuitous opportunity to help bridge the gulfs that separate the haves from the have-nots, or will they further divide the community? Carefully answering these questions and meticulously planning New Orleans' reconstruction are inextricably interwoven into the quest to define the future of New Orleans.

The city of Chicago once faced a similar crisis. After the Great Fire destroyed a significant portion of the city in 1871, and Chicago's inability to sufficiently answer the vital questions facing the city's reconstruction plans that should have benefited all citizens. Missed opportunities should not be repeated in New Orleans.

On April 2, 2006, the City Colleges of Chicago's TV station, WYCC, the largest education-focused public broadcasting entity in Illinois, aired a documentary on the construction building trades. The documentary began with the history of rebuilding Chicago after the Great Fire of 1871, explaining how the exclusion of some ethnic groups from the building trades left a segregated city that helped define Chicago for the 20th century and into the 21st century. One of Chicago's challenges for the 21st century is still how to ensure racial and gender equity in the building trades.

Although Hurricane Katrina resulted in the tragic loss of many more lives than were lost in the Chicago fire, both events were destructive and presented opportunities for new growth.[2] Approximately 78,000 homes in New Orleans were destroyed[3] and a year after Katrina, less than 50 percent of those citizens who fled the city had returned.[4] In comparison, the Chicago fire leveled 18,000 buildings and left a third of the city's residents homeless,[5] without resources and without jobs.

Thousands of skilled and unskilled craftsmen were needed to rebuild Chicago after the Great Fire of 1871. Coupled with the need to meet the construction demands of the Chicago-hosted World's Fair in 1893, thousands of immigrants from Europe were brought in to fill numerous craftsmen positions. Those immigrants, in turn, helped their brothers, uncles and cousins settle in Chicago and gain employment. From these sanguine and familial groups, trade associations were formed, and two unlikely events—the Great Fire and the World's Fair—that occurred within a short time span helped establish the foundation for the development of construction trades in Chicago.

Blacks, Hispanics, and women were minimally included in these early associations and, as time went on, the "old boy" networks hardened, jobs were passed to family members, and women and minorities were excluded from participation in the building and construction trades industry in Chicago. The city is still trying to rectify the inequities that arose during this time.

The dearth of apprentice opportunities for blacks, Hispanics and women entering the construction trades has been amplified because of the projected cost of current public and private construction projects in the Chicago region. The greater Chicago area will have an infusion of money available for construction; including $10 billion a year for the next decade to complete public works projects such as the O'Hare Modernization Program, the Illinois Tollway Congestion Relief Plan, and the Chicago Skyway and Local Freeways Rebuilding Projects.[6]

The impact of the missed opportunity to include minorities in the construction trades can be measured financially. Between 1980 and 2000, the black community could have earned $5.9 billion (in 2005 dollars) in gross income had black male participation in the construction sector been equal to their representation in the Cook County labor force.[7] Each year, the number of black males missing from the trades increases (from 4,032 missing in 1980 to 5,148 missing in 2000).[8] This impact is replicated in other cities. Throughout America, blacks and women are being deprived of billions of dollars when it comes to fair employment and access in the construction trade industry.

What would have been the economic impact on these communities without racial and gender discrimination? Would there be less poverty if more work opportunities were available? Chicago communities with the highest unemployment rates also tend to have higher poverty rates and a greater percentage of minority populations. The five community areas with the highest unemployment rates in 2006 were all predominantly black communities with 32 to 56 percent of residents living below poverty level. In comparison, four of the five community areas with the lowest unemployment levels were predominantly white communities with less than 10 percent of residents living below poverty level.[9] Ghettos exist because poverty exists. We have drive-by shootings because of poverty. We have children not graduating from high school and not going to college because we have poverty. Most important, poverty is a direct result of unemployment. Decades of poverty can cause men and women to reach the point where they no longer have the desire to work. This is the place where the community college plays an important role as an advocate for the unemployed. Construction companies do not have to go to Wisconsin or Indiana to find workers; they can hire Chicago residents. It is in the city's best interest to hire residents in neighborhoods where unemployment is high.

Successful workforce development is a system of stakeholders, businesses, community colleges, unions and community organizations and legislators who clearly identify (1) the work that must be accomplished; (2) a cohort of entry-level or incumbent workers who need to be trained; (3) a training curricula; (4) specified jobs to be filled; (4) revenue to support the hard and soft program components; and (5) the will and the desire to hire people once they are successfully trained regardless of the ethnicity or gender.

City Colleges of Chicago became a proactive service stakeholder by working with leaders from the building associations, politicians, and trade associations to increase minority participation in the construction industry at both the worker and the contractor levels.

Through partnerships with trades associations, City Colleges has established a panoply of short-term apprenticeship prep programs in carpentry, bricklaying, cement masonry, plumbing, and welding that are designed to prepare minorities to succeed in the construction industry. Additionally, full apprenticeship programs leading to the associate of applied science degrees are being offered in:

1. Elevator Constructors Union.
2. Painters Union District 14.
3. Com-Ed Overhead Lineman's.

4. International Union of Operating Engineers' Local 150 Materials Testing.

These combination trade/degree programs also articulate to the baccalaureate level, providing construction workers a career path from laborer to project manager, or company owner. The oldest of these programs, the Electrical Construction Technologies program, enrolled 562 trainees in fiscal year 2007, an increase from 430 trainees in fiscal year 2006.[10] The valued construction trade partners associated with these combination trade/degree programs are providing opportunities and ensuring access for ethnic groups and women to their respective trade unions. These valued partners understand the quintessential role that trade unions must play to ensure a level playing field and fair access to their apprenticeship programs.

Through partnerships with the Building and Construction Trades Contractors, jobs are being guaranteed for program graduates. Local politicians have supported ordinances and legislation to provide contractors a reduction on their bid price if they hire graduates of City Colleges of Chicago construction programs.

Despite these efforts, the question still looms: "Will Chicago and New Orleans train portentous numbers of local women and minority residents to avoid having to recruit and train thousands of transient workers from surrounding states and ensure ethnic and gender diversity in the trades?" If Chicago and New Orleans want to create ethnic and gender diversity, they will work to change the political, cultural, and social fabric of their respective regions.

In 2006, City Colleges of Chicago gave testimony during a Congressional Black Caucus hearing at the National Association for Equal Opportunity in Higher Education (NAFEO) annual conference in New Orleans. I stated to the Congressmen, "You might be asking at about this point in my presentation, 'Why is Chicago, the City Colleges of Chicago, here talking about Louisiana?' The bottom line is that community colleges throughout America stand ready to develop models for partnerships with local building trades."

I then added: "New Orleans is blessed to have the Louisiana Community and Technical College System. It can be central to the reconstruction efforts in this state. Prior to Katrina, the system's enrollment had a record 50,920 students in the fall semester of 2004.[11]" After experiencing a 40 percent decrease in enrollment following Hurricanes Katrina and Rita, the system is rebounding quickly, with some of its colleges experiencing record enrollments in Fall 2007.[12] The community college system in Louisiana is poised to grow because it trained local residents who will, in turn, rebuild Louisiana. However, the system will need support in order for this reconstruction initiative to succeed.

Funding will be needed to train a skilled workforce estimated to reach 30,000 to 40,000 persons. Further, the federal government and state and local elected officials need to provide the basic guarantees that New Orleans will be rebuilt in its entirety, rather than in a piecemeal fashion where only economically advantaged neighborhoods will survive.

Ordinances should be passed to provide incentives for hiring minority and women graduates of construction training programs. Builders need to support the Louisiana Community & Technical College System's efforts by making a commitment to hire and promote program graduates and by stressing that in Louisiana, community colleges should play a central role in rebuilding Louisiana. By working together, we can rebuild the Louisiana region of America and ensure that women and minorities are included in and benefit from that process. For our part, City Colleges of Chicago commits to supporting these efforts in every possible way.

(Annotated from a speech given at the 31st NAFEO National Conference on Blacks in Higher Education for the U.S. Congressional Black Caucus Field Hearing on the Impact of Hurricanes Katrina and Rita on Historically Black Colleges and Universities New Orleans, Louisiana March 23, 2006.)

END NOTES

[1] National Public Radio (2005): *An American History of Disaster and Response.* Retrieved January 15, 2008, from http://www.npr.org.

[2] It is estimated that between 200 and 300 people died in the Chicago fire of 1871. Source: Chicago Historical Society & Northwestern University (1996). The Ruined City. The Great Chicago Fire and the Web of Memory. Retrieved January 15, 2008, from http://www.chicagohs.org/fire/.
The count of lives lost in Louisiana after Katrina is 1,577. Source: Koch, K. (2007). *Katrina-ravaged, Gulf Coast struggling 2 years later.* Retrieved January 15, 2008, from http://www.cnn.com/.

[3] Vince, G. & Hecht, J. (2006). *Hurricane Katrina: One year later.* Retrieved January 16, 2008, from http://www.newscientist.com/home.ns.

[4] Ibid.

[5] Sawislak, K. (2005): *Fire of 1871.* Encyclopedia of Chicago. Retrieved January 16, 2008, from http://www.encyclopedia.chicagohistory.org/.

[6] Taylor, T. S. (2006): *The Pathway to Apprenticeship: Roadblocks to Registration of Minorities and Women in Building Trade Union Apprenticeship Training Programs in Northeastern Illinois.*

[7] Taylor, T. S. & Bilginsoy, C. (2006): *Economic Impact Special Report. Black Male Participation in Cook County's Construction Sector: Looking Back to the Future.*

[8] Ibid.

[9] Lower West Side had the third lowest unemployment rate, but was predominantly Hispanic with 27 percent of residents living below the poverty level. Sources: Illinois Department of Employment Security (2007). Annual Average Unemployment Rates by Chicago Community Area: 2000 – 2006 (unpublished, unofficial data).
Census 2000 data by Chicago Community Area. Retrieved January 15, 2008, from http://www.nd.edu/~chifacts/chicago.html.

[10] CCC Program Profile at Daley College (FY 2007). This program is only offered at Daley College.

[11] Louisiana Community and Technical College System, Office of Institutional Research. *LCTCS Enrollment Trends: Fall 1999 to Fall 2006.* Retrieved January 15, 2008, from http://www.lctcs.net/about-research.asp.

[12] Louisiana Community and Technical College System (September 7, 2007). *LCTCS Fall Enrollment Numbers Reflect System-Wide Growth. Press Release.* Retrieved January 15, 2008, from http://www.lctcs.net/news.asp?articleID=261.

Historically Black Colleges and Universities: Cultivating Global Citizenship

Dr. George T. French, Jr.
President, Miles College

Ideology of Internationalization

The isolationism that dominated American foreign policy during the 19th, and parts of the 20th centuries has given way to the ideology of internationalism. Modern political, economic, and technological triggering mechanisms required that the United States revisit the sociopolitical world theory rooted in its formative years. President George Washington expressed the view that foreign entanglements, except for purposes of trade, should be entered into with hesitancy. However, a chronology of major happenings spanning through the 20th century—World War I, World War II and its aftermath, the Cold War—and the nascent years of the 21st century which brought with it terrorist attacks on the World Trade Center on September 11, 2001 brought about a theoretical departure from isolationism to one of international interdependence. As such, Historically Black Colleges and Universities (HBCUs) must prepare themselves and their students to be viable participants in a global society.

Although the formal study of international relations began in earnest during the start of the 20th century, cosmopolitanism, a principal cognitive structure of internationalism, gained traction during the Enlightenment with philosophers such as Immanuel Kant. This was an era marked by the rise of capitalism and worldwide trade, expanding empires whose reach encompassed the globe. The emergence of a notion of human rights and a philosophical focus on human reason was also taking root. Kant's works *Perpetual Peace* (1795) and an *Idea for a Universal History with a Cosmopolitan Purpose* (1784), uphold a universal civil society in which people are viewed as the end themselves, rather than a means to an end. Kant supported the idea of world citizenship.[1]

Contemporary international study has primarily focused on globalization. Economist, professor and editor of the *Harvard Business Review*, Theodore Levitt coined the term globalization in 1983.[2] The term was used initially to describe the emergence of products sold around the world at standardized, low-prices. However, ubiquitous popular discourse has resulted in a variety of meanings for the term globalization. In the most general sense, the word is often used to refer to the worldwide spread of capitalism, commerce and advanced technology.[3] Globalization actually refers to the:

> "Supranational, no isolationist outlook with other conceptions of internationalism, it differs from most of them in its emphasis on international power and influence rather than cooperation. The terms refer primarily to the U.S. policy of global engagement aimed at expanding its political influence and economic markets, but it is also applied to the Soviet Union's efforts to extend its own sphere of influence during the Cold War." (Ibid).

Globalization centers on capitalism and survival of the economic fittest; this contradicts popular culture's use of the word to mean interdependence and collaboration.

With such ambiguity defining this phenomenon, for purposes of discussion it is imperative to offer a uniform concept to function as the foundational thesis throughout the article, thus global (as opposed to globalization) and internationalization will be used interchangeably as synonyms to refer to the political, social, educational, technological and economic changes in human activity that result in interdependence or the need for interdependence, crowning in the synthesis of global interests for the purposes of sharing, promoting, and/or preserving national interests.

Necessity For Internationalization of HBCUs

African Americans are sensitive to the concept of globalization because it isolates and for many advanced countries means trade with Europe while Africa is exploited or not included. Globalization is beholden to the concept of *laissez faire* and outsourcing, which historically has subjugated, or excluded those of African descent, other ethnic and racial minorities, and the economically poor. It leaves little room for government intervention, which has been essential for acquiring rights and inclusion of marginalized groups. While globalization has some positive outcomes for society and African Americans, internationalization is more comprehensive in approach, focusing on world interdependence which includes social, economic, political, educational, and technological components and thus should be a focus for HBCUs.

When the question is raised as to why a campus should internationalize, a publication by the American Council on Education (ACE) titled *Educating Americans for a World in Flux*, is often referenced. The question is answered by stating:

> "*The world in which most adult Americans grew to maturity no longer exists. The Cold War is over. The domestic economy is global. The 'melting pot' is boiling over. Our world is in flux. The approach of the 21st century foreshadows not simply a new millennium, but a completely new and different globe...Superpower confrontation has been replaced by regional instability. Jobs lost at home reappear abroad. Industrial accidents spread pollution across borders. Public health problems vault oceans. Goods and services flow freely across borders and among great trading blocks. American graduates must compete with their peers from overseas. In truth, the line separating 'foreign' from 'domestic' is much harder to define today than it was yesterday, and much of our domestic success depends on events taking place elsewhere.*" (American Council on Education, 1995, p. 3)

Some larger universities and colleges have engaged in internationalizing their campuses for decades. International studies as an enterprise at American institutions of higher education began to expand at some large, majority colleges and universities during the years immediately following World War II. The number of individuals earning a Ph.D. in international studies more than doubled between the years 1948 to 1951 from 100 to 225 respectively. Doubling again between 1955 and 1965, and then occured again by 1970.

Scholars divide the internationalization of U.S. higher education into two phases, the *first wave* and *second wave*. "The first wave is a direct outgrowth of the World War II experience, while the second wave reflects the acceleration of global intercourse that marked the final two decades of the last century." (Merx, 2003, p. 6) Several factors marking the *first wave* are responsible for metamorphosis of international education at these majority higher education institutions: the large number of foreign students seeking to matriculate through majority institutions, foreign aid, study abroad programs, and foreign language area studies. The *second wave* of internationalization started during the mid-1980s and through the late 1990s. This wave is defined by accelerated economic interaction, increased access and usage of the Internet, the end of the Cold War and the subsequent emergence of the United States as having the world's strongest military.[4]

I argue that a *third* wave has emerged. This *wave* has a period of demarcation immediately post the September 11, 2001 terrorist attacks. This *wave* is underscored by an emerging China and Japan; territorial, religious and ethnic tensions in and with parts of the Middle East, and clashes with North Korea. As such, the United States' local, state, and federal governments have turned to academia for answers on how to navigate through the process of resolving these pressing issues. The dependence on academia to provide insight is not new. For numerous societal shifts, academia has operated as the incubator for critical thinking, requiring examination of less obvious meanings, exploring reasons from different viewpoints of the same event, and assimilating a wide array of information into a complex, dynamic perspective. As such, academia has functioned, and continues to function, as the ideal forum for the study of internationalization concepts which can be universally embraced.

HBCUs cannot afford to fail our communities by enabling them to global incompetence. To do so would impede African-American global progress, career opportunities, relegate communities to careers bound by borders, and deprive our communities of the confidence it takes to compete in this globally focused society. To not cultivate global citizenship in African-American communities would hinder us from contributing our philosophies and ideals as they pertain to how local, state, and federal governments, and business communities interact with other countries. HBCUs produce a large number of the black intelligentsia who make up African-American communities. We must be sure that our mark is imprinted upon this global intersection in history.

HBCUs offer America and especially the government, officially responsible for creating a spectrum of policies in relation to other countries, an invaluable resource. The National Center for Education Statistics in its 1996 study on HBCUs titled, *Historically Black Colleges and Universities: 1976 to 1994*, found a 21 percent increase of students at HBCUs between 1976 and 1994. Eighty-five percent of the nation's black physicians, 80 percent of African-American federal judges, 75 percent of blacks earning Ph.Ds, 50 percent of black business executives and elected officials were educated at HBCUs. For the past 150 years, HBCUs have prepared African Americans for the economic, social, and political challenges of America.

Nearly one-third of all African Americans who receive college degrees earn them from HBCUs. This fact is even more pronounced when it is noted that HBCUs enroll only about 16 percent of African-American students. The majority of African Americans with Ph.D. degrees, medical degrees, law degrees, federal judgeships, and officer rank in the U.S. military did their undergraduate studies at HBCUs.[5] It is imperative for small liberal arts colleges, and all HBCUs to make our students globally conscious so that they may act as a conduit in making our communities globally conscious.

We are at a critical juncture in history in which perspectives of people of color must be included in policy formulation at all levels, more so now than ever given that most of the immediate and major tensions are in the Middle East, a region in which many people of color live. When, or if these Middle East conflicts are resolved, America must prepare herself to address other conflicts that will occur during this internationalization process, and since people of color are the majority in the global community (i.e., the combined number of people of color in India, the Middle East, Africa and South America), it is likely that the need will continue to exist. Having phenotypic similarities, as well as similarities in customs and practices, African Americans are ideal to represent America's diplomatic core abroad and help formulate policy at all levels of government. For this reason, not only is there a need for increased government support of international education because of the current international shifts, there is also a profound need to fund international education at HBCUs because of what HBCUs are inherently, the communities which HBCUs serve, and the present and potential conflicts with countries predominately populated by people of color.

In addition to making contributions in shaping global thought, HBCUs are in a position to shape official American policy by functioning as a resource for the Intelligence Community (IC). The IC is a federation of agencies and organizations that work separately and together to conduct intelligence activities relevant to foreign relations and the protection of the national security of the United States. IC members are: Air Force Intelligence, Army Intelligence, Central Intelligence Agency, Coast Guard Intelligence, Defense Intelligence Agency, Department of Energy, Department of Homeland Security, Department of State, Department of the Treasury, Drug Enforcement Administration, Federal Bureau of Investigation, Marine Corps Intelligence, National Geospatial-Intelligence Agency, National Reconnaissance Office, National Security Agency, and Navy Intelligence. Although it is imperative that HBCUs maintain the integrity of their missions to independently educate and not become beholden to any particular government agency, creating a partnership with the IC or one of its members could result in an HBCU strengthening its institution by way of government relationships, and receiving funds for buildings and programs.

Internationalizing our campuses would be beneficial on many levels. First, it provides our students, and thus our communities, with a worldly perspective and an awareness of other cultures. Second, it would prepare our students to meaningfully compete for national and international careers. Third, it would create an environment more welcoming for international study, likely attracting more international students and in turn more financial resources for the institution. Fourth, HBCUs would make themselves competitive to receive and create funding opportunities from the local, state and federal governments. The latter two points are particularly relevant to small liberal arts colleges in that internationalizing our campuses could realistically increase funding opportunities by way of enrollment, international enterprise, and government partnerships Additional ways in which internationalizing a campus generates income are: national security program development and training to be used in other countries; delivery of distance learning courses for students outside of the United States; partnerships with local and international corporations; and contracts to provide special training programs for faculty, leaders, and business managers in other countries.[6]

Internationalization at Miles College

Traditionally, HBCUs and in particular small ones have not had the resources, or the luxury to expand outside the parameters of a routine academic curriculum. However, the compelling need for a global perspective has been heightened by increasing ethnic, social, and custom diversity; nuclear proliferation; illegal immigration; and an escalating Middle East conflict. Thus, various United States' entities have arrived at the awareness that they are deficient in global competence and that they have a need for help in addressing these escalating issues. Although internationalization is unchartered territory for many HBCUs, there are some examples of success. Visionary, bold, and resilient leadership with insight and foresight of the characteristics and direction of our society are required when embarking upon the goal of internationalizing an institution.

Miles College, a small liberal arts colleges located in Birmingham, Alabama, has formalized this objective by creating an International Studies and Public Policy program within the Division of Social and Behavioral Sciences in the Spring of 2007. Although still in its formative stages, the program offers Arabic, in addition to Spanish and French. Miles has hosted a Diplomat-in-Residence from the Department of State to inform its students about various international career opportunities. Also, through the Department of State, the College applied for and received a 2007-2008 Fulbright scholar-in-residence professor from India, who teaches courses related to Southeast Asia and India. The current Fulbright professor is one of many that the college has hosted. Symposia focusing on global topics are routinely held at the college. Recently discussed issues include: Gandhi and King: War, Peace, and Conflict Resolution; Global Issues: Impact of Multicultural Organizations on National Identities; Developing a New Consciousness in a Global Society; Global Challenges Seminar: Insight into International Studies; India-Pakistan Relations and the United States: Post-September 11th; Democracy in the Middle East: The Experience of Egypt; and Racial Struggles at Home and Abroad. These and numerous other lectures are held on campus to expose students, faculty, and staff to international issues.

Miles College is also a member of several internationally affiliated organizations. The institution is currently a member of the United Nations Association—Greater Birmingham Chapter and Sister Cities, Inc., an organization initiated by President Eisenhower to involve individuals and organized groups at all levels of society in international citizen diplomacy. Additionally, Miles is a member of the College Consortium for International Studies as well a member of the Alabama Conference for International Programs.

There is a growing study abroad program at Miles. Students in the Honors Curriculum travel abroad annually. Furthermore, students have travelled to the Dominican Republic through the college's partnership with the Black Colleges and Universities consortium. Middlesex University in England has been another destination of study for Miles' young scholars.

Additionally, Miles College has amalgamated internationalization objectives with other institutions. In 2004 Miles College and the University of Malawi Chancellor College entered into a Memorandum of Understanding which has resulted in the exchange of students and faculty for the purposes of strengthening coursework, research and cultural understanding. Miles College is currently successfully executing a Memorandum of Understanding with the United States Agency for International Development allowing for the opportunity to assist in global programs, and a Memorandum of Agreement with the United Negro College Fund Special Programs that facilitates study abroad opportunities.

All of these internationalization components combined are foundational in the college's implementation of a minor in International Studies, expanding into a major, and thereafter a School of International Studies and Public Policy for which the land has already been purchased, buttressed by a strong capital campaign. The proposed School will function as a Southeastern regional hub for a well-rounded International Studies and Public Policy program. It will function as an institutional archetype for Miles College, other colleges and universities, the United States and the global community to engage in the study, discourse and application of internationalization. The aim of the School is to be a comprehensive academy in which students, faculty, public-policy makers and scholars will convene for critical study, policy application, and global intelligence inquiry as it relates to international issues identification;

issue commitments; policy formulation; policy implementation and policy evaluation.

Approaches for Internationalizing our Colleges

Internationalization of a campus is a tremendous undertaking which requires an institutional ideological paradigm shift. This is an evolutionary process in which institutional leadership, students, faculty and staff must examine and redefine how they perceive themselves. We must begin to see internationalization not simply as what we do, but an integral part of who we are as institutions. We must begin to look at the world through the lens of a global community inclusive of, but also beyond our colleges, and in doing so view ourselves as a vital part of this global community. Starting from the cafeteria staff to the college cashier, to the faculty, each has a role to play, regardless to the size or function. For instance, the cafeteria staff may decide to serve a traditional Brazilian dish, or the cashier may decide to display currency from South Korea, faculty members may choose to present international studies articles at various conferences.

To be sure, the commitment, and tangible and intangible mandate to globalize must come from the president of the institution. The president of the college is responsible for putting forth the platform and has the power inherent in the office, requiring and inspiring other units to follow. A leadership directive must be espoused by the president as a proclamation to become global. A serious-minded executive leader must effectively communicate internationalization as a primary objective for 21st century academic governance. The president accordingly must provide administrators responsible for contriving globalizing the campus authority that is institutionalized as opposed to ad hoc and evanescent. These administrators must have the power of centralization and decentralization of existing and proposed college international activity. In doing so, the unmistakable intent of the college to internationalize will be branded.

A practical first approach to internationalization, particularly at a small liberal arts college or university is to do an initial assessment of current global activity on campus. A study of the campus may reveal a plethora of faculty, administrators, and students engaged in some form of international activity; for example, engaging international students, immigrants in the community, foreign language learners, and study abroad participants in more activities on campus. A survey of these individuals and their skills and experiences may highlight plausible contributions and act as a cadre of internationalization accomplishments. This is a starting point for a modest international studies program that can parlay into a comprehensive program.

Internationalizing the curriculum is another component to a strategic approach. Examining current curriculum for international tenants is a start. An initial review of existing courses to determine whether they can be revised or strengthened to reflect global content is essential. New courses need to be in concert with a campus' objective of why it is internationalizing.

Study abroad programs are another means to becoming global. According to the Institute for International Education's 2006 *Open Doors* report and the U.S. Department of Education Statistics, African-American students make up only 3 percent of study abroad participants. Our students need to be exposed to available study abroad opportunities and earn college credit for study abroad. The Paul Simon Study Abroad Foundation Act has been proposed to help ameliorate the number of study abroad participants. The act focuses on providing funding opportunities to enable study abroad participation to increase from around 200,000 to 1 million students annually within 10 years. (National Association of Foreign Student Advisors, 2007) Currently, the act is in the Senate and has been referred to the Committee on Foreign Relations. (The Library of Congress, 2007)

Several study abroad challenges face small HBCUs, and colleges in general: interests, funding, and parental disapproval of leaving stateside. Observing international activities on campus will pique student interest to international travel possibilities, informing students that travel abroad is no longer only for the wealthy or elite, as well as making them aware that study abroad will give them worldly exposure to other cultures. Additionally, colleges must provide funding resource information for students interested in studying aboard. And as far as parental support, parents must be involved. The parents of interested students must be actively sought out, and they must be included in the total process.

Smaller institutions may not have the capacity or be able to bear legal liabilities associated with study abroad programs, thus encouraging relationships with consortia. These partnerships are synergistic and symbiotic relationships that are fundamental to becoming an effective global citizen. International higher education consortia can be the roadmap to many avenues for smaller institutions to have access to services such as courses, faculty, and study abroad programs and in return smaller HBCUs offer diversity with respect to grant and funding opportunities requiring such.

Using external consultants is another key strategy. Quality outside counsel is useful in providing direction for internationalization across a campus: internationalization of curriculum; study abroad opportunities for students; internationalizing student affairs and academic units; and integrating international students, international visiting scholars and professors, and researchers into campus life. Internationalization consultants conduct an internationalization audit and advise each institution based upon its unique set of needs, opportunities, strengths and weaknesses. (Ellingboe, 2003, pp. 22-27) An internal advisory committee familiar with the college must also be created as a means to demonstrate inclusiveness, an interdisciplinary perspective and openness in this monumental process.

Conclusion

Post-cold war events have ushered our country into an era where we are faced with increasing diversity, nuclear proliferation, and an escalating Middle East conflict. We now live in a society where human activity and engagement is no longer isolated by borders or ethnicity. Internationalization is here to stay and there is evidence that its momentum, although slow at times, will not retard. Small HBCUs, and in essence, no HBCU need rob our students and communities of preparation to be competitive in the internationalized world. To not heed the call to internationalize to some degree will essentially make an institution irrelevant in the very near future. Our students need to be globalized to help enhance international understanding and perpetuate world peace, and compete successfully in global enterprise. Our government needs HBCUs to internationalize to produce knowledgable individuals to create and support United States foreign policy and diplomacy. Small HBCUs need not believe that we do not have a role to play. To the contrary, since our institutions are smaller we are more so amendable for transitioning our campuses to be internationalized; we have fewer layers of bureaucracy which is helpful when implementing an ideology of such magnitude. The terrain of internationalizing our campuses may be rough and cumbersome, but in the world in which we now live, it is no longer optional.

ENDNOTES

[1] Kleingeld, P. & Brown, E. (2006). *Cosmopolitanism*. Retrieved October 8, 2006, from Stanford Encyclopedia of Philosophy Web site: http://plato.stanford.edu/entries/cosmopolitanism/; Rohmann, C. (1999). *A World Of Ideas: A Dictionary Of Important Theories, Concepts, Beliefs And Thinkers*. New York: Ballantine Books. pp 198-199.

[2] Scheuerman, W. (2006). *Globalization*. Retrieved October 2, 2006, from Stanford Encyclopedia of Philosophy Web site: http://plato.stanford.edu/entries/globalization/.

[3] Ibid.

[4] Merkx, G.W. (2003). *The Two Waves Of Internationalization In U.S. Higher Education*. International Educator. 12(1), 6.

[5] Gray, W.H. (1997). *The Case For All Black Colleges*. Retrieved January 2003, from Education Information Resource Center Web site: http://www.eric.ed.gov/resources/ericreview/vol5no3/black.html.

[6] Green, M. p.16.

Contributors

Dr. Everette J. Freeman was named the eighth president of Albany State University on September 7, 2005 and officially took office on October 10. Prior to coming to Albany, Freeman served four years as senior vice president and provost at the University of Indianapolis. He previously was the executive assistant to the president at Tennessee State University, where he served as interim vice president for University Relations and Development.

Freeman served as chairman of the board of the Indiana Lung Association and was a board member of organizations including La Plaza (IN) federation of Latino organizations, Indianapolis Private Industry Council, Crossroads of America Council of Boy Scouts, and HealthNet Incorporated in Indianapolis. He is a trustee on the board of Antioch College and currently is a board member of community organizations including Albany (GA) and Lee County (GA) Chamber of Commerce, United Way of Albany, Georgia Partnership for Excellence in Education, Albany Tomorrow, Inc. and Albany/Dougherty Community Partnership for Education and Communities in Schools. He has received several local, state, national and international awards and honors; notably, he was named a George Cadbury Scholar at Fircroft College in England in 1970-1971 and a Fellow of the Society of Values in Higher Education from 1985 to present. He received the 2004 appreciation award from the National League of Cities, NBC-LEO in Indianapolis.

Dr. Freeman received his bachelor's degree in sociology/economics from Antioch College in 1972, a master's degree in labor and industrial relations from the University of Illinois in 1974 and an Ed.D. in education foundations from Rutgers University in 1983. He also holds a certificate from the Institute for Educational Leadership at Harvard University and a certificate in Economics from Fircroft College in Birmingham, England.

Dr. George T. French, Jr. is the president of Miles College. He has served in several leadership capacities during his more than 10 years stay at Miles. As director of Institutional Planning & Development, he was the Chief Development Officer and directed the offices of Development, Alumni Affairs, Federal Contracts & Grants, Title III, Institutional Research & Effectiveness, Congressional Relations, Public Relations and Promotions and long-range planning.

CONTRIBUTORS

Dr. French is a National Kellogg Fellow; a 2005 graduate of Leadership Birmingham; member of the Judicial Council Justice for the Christian Methodist Episcopal Church (C.M.E.); board member, YMCA Western Branch; Phi Alpha Delta Law Fraternity; National Bar Association; Governor's Commission of Historically Black Colleges; vice chairman of the Singleton Foundation; Alpha Phi Alpha Fraternity; Rotary Club of Birmingham, and co-author of "Miles College, The First 100 Years".

During the administration of the late Dr. Albert J. H. Sloan, III, Dr. French led Miles' largest and most successful major Capital Campaign Fund Drive, Determining Our Destiny, which raised over $12 million. Dr. French has also been responsible for oversight of campus renovation and new construction projects exceeding $24 million.

Dr. French received a bachelor's degree from the University of Louisville, a law degree from Miles College, and a Ph.D. from Jackson State University.

Dr. William R. Harvey has served with distinction as president of Hampton University since 1978. He has created a monumental legacy during his more than twenty-five year tenure—one of the longest tenure of any sitting president of a college or university in the country.

Dr. William R. Harvey's leadership is reflected in the growth and quality of the University's student population, academic programs, physical facilities, and financial base. During Dr. Harvey's tenure as president, the student enrollment at Hampton University has increased from approximately 2,700 students to over 6,300. Moreover, the average SAT score of entering freshmen has increased approximately 300 points.

Dr. Harvey's commitment to expansion and innovation in academic programs has resulted in 76 new academic programs being implemented under his watch. Some of these new thrusts include undergraduate programs in Computer Science, Marine Science, Entrepreneurship, Chemical, Electrical and Computer Engineering, Airway Science, Emergency Medical Assistance Management; graduate programs in Business Administration (MBA), Applied Mathematics and doctoral degrees in Physics, Pharmacy, Physical Therapy, and Nursing.

Dr. Harvey's financial leadership is indicated in the financial growth and stability Hampton has achieved during his twenty-eight years as president. The University has balanced its budget and achieved a surplus during each of those years. The endowment, which stood at $29 million when he became president, now exceeds $200 million. The University's first capital fundraising campaign in 1979 had a goal of $30,000,000. That campaign raised $46.4 million. The most recent campaign had a goal of $200 million and raised $264 million.

Dr. Harvey received his bachelor's degree from Talladega College and his doctorate in college administration from Harvard University.

Dr. Julianne Malveaux is the 15th president of Bennett College for Women. Recognized for her progressive and insightful observations, she is also an economist, author and commentator. Dr. Malveaux's contributions to the public dialogue on issues such as race, culture, gender, and their economic impacts, are shaping public opinion in 21st century America.

As a writer and a syndicated columnist, her writing appears regularly in *USA Today*, *Black Issues in Higher Education*, *Ms. Magazine*, *Essence* magazine, and the *Progressive*. Her weekly columns appear in numerous newspapers across the country including the *Los Angeles Times*, the *Charlotte Observer*, the *New Orleans Tribune*, the *Detroit Free Press*, and the *San Francisco Examiner*.

In addition to her columns and media appearances, Dr. Malveaux is an accomplished author and editor. Her academic work is included in numerous papers, studies, and publications. She is the editor of *Voices of Vision: African American Women on the Issues* (1996); the co-editor of *Slipping Through the Cracks: The Status of Black Women* (1986), and recently co-edited *The Paradox of Loyalty: An African American Response to the War on Terrorism* (2002). She is the author of two column anthologies: *Sex, Lies, and Stereotypes: Perspectives of a Mad Economist* (1994), *Wall Street, Main Street, and the Side Street: A Mad Economist Takes a Stroll* (1999). She is most recently the co-author of *Unfinished Business: A Democrat and A Republican Take On the 10 Most Important Issues Women Face* (2002).

Dr. Malveaux received her bachelor's and master's degrees in economics from Boston College and earned a Ph.D in economics from MIT. A native San Franciscan, she is the president and CEO of Last Word Productions, Inc. a multimedia production company headquartered in Washington, DC, and currently resides in Greensboro, NC.

Dr. Trudie Kibbe Reed is Bethune-Cookman University's fifth president and the first woman to serve in this capacity since the institution's founder, Dr. Mary McLeod Bethune. Dr. Reed assumed the presidency of Bethune-Cookman University on August 16, 2004 after a successful career in higher education as both a former college president and a high ranking administrator within The United Methodist Church.

Dr. Reed was confirmed by the White House to serve on the U.S. President's White House Advisory Board for Historically Black Colleges and Universities. During that time, she consulted with the U.S. Secretary of Education on issues related to HBCUs. As a former chairperson of the Foundation for the MidSouth, Dr. Reed worked to improve conditions of citizens in the area of literacy, education and leadership development.

Dr. Reed currently serves on the UNCF member institutions board, the United Methodist Foundation of the Central Council of Finance and Administration. She was recently selected by the governor of Florida on the State Voluntarism Commission. Dr. Reed is a member of the Daytona Beach Chamber of Commerce, Rotary International, the Futures Foundation for Volusia County Schools, and the United Way Board.

Dr. Reed received a bachelor's degree in sociology and a master's degree in social work (MSW) from the University of Texas at Austin. She also received a master's degree and a doctoral degree from Columbia University in adult and higher education.

Dr. William E. Spriggs became chair of the Department and a professor of Economics at Howard University in Washington, DC in December 2005. Before that, Dr. Spriggs was at the Economic Policy Institute as senior fellow, having returned there in 2004.

From 1988 to 2004, he was executive director of the National Urban League's Institute for Opportunity and Equality, where among other duties he was editor of the *State of Black America 1999*, and led research on pay equity that won the NUL 2001 Winn Newman Award from the National Committee on Pay Equity.

Before working at the National Urban League, Dr. Spriggs held various positions in government service during the Clinton Administration: in 1993 and 1994 he led the staff of the National Commission for Employment Policy, and in 1997 and 1998 he worked at the Department of Commerce, where he worked on the federal response to the *Adarand v. Pena* decision.

He served as a senior economist for the Democratic staff of the Joint Economic Committee of the U.S. Congress from 1994 to 1997, where, among other things, he worked on the passage of the increase in the minimum wage and to prevent legislative efforts to roll back affirmative action in federal procurement. He is a past-board member and president of the National Economic Association—the professional organization of Black economists

Dr. Spriggs received a bachelor's degree, *cum laude,* from Williams College, and Ph.D. from the University of Wisconsin, Madison.

Dr. Wayne Watson is the chancellor of the City Colleges of Chicago. appointed chancellor in 1998, he immediately began instituting the changes he saw as needed to achieve the excellence in education he so passionately wanted to bring to Chicago's diverse community. Prior to his appointment, he served as president of Kennedy-King College and Harold Washington College.

Dr. Watson's professional dedication to excellence in education aligns with his strong commitment to community service. He currently serves on the board of trustees of Northwestern University, board of directors of the American Association of Community Colleges, National Association for Equal Opportunity in Higher Education, Windy City Harvest, the Fantus Health Center Board, the Capital Campaign Leadership Committee for the Institute of Puerto Rican Arts and Culture and as a volunteer to the Capital Campaign for the DuSable Museum of African American History.

Dr. Watson takes great pride in having worked as a senior consultant to Alex Haley. In this position, he reviewed and validated the research methodology Haley went on to use in writing his international bestseller, *Roots*.

Dr. Watson's higher education started at Joliet Junior College. From there he went on to Northwestern University where he earned his bachelor's master's, and doctoral degrees.

Appendices

The information in the appendices contains data on NAFEO member institutions that is derived from the *2007 NAFEO Annual Membership Survey* and the U.S. Department of Education's National Center on Education Statistics (NCES) through its Integrated Postsecondary Education Data System (IPEDS).

The second section of the appendix contains data on select NAFEO member institutions that was gathered in the *2007 Annual NAFEO Membership Survey*. This section includes information on the institutions' curricula, special programs and collections, centers of excellence, research capacities, and community initiatives.

In 2007, NAFEO re-launched its annual membership survey. The 43-question survey was sent electronically to each institution's office of the president/chancellor in October 2007. A total of 40 institutions responded to the survey, which consisted of 12 sections. The questions were fill-in-the blank, yes/no, and open-ended. The sections of the survey included: curricula data, enrollment, student achievement, tuition and financial aid, endowment, centers of excellence, technological capacity, faculty data, goods produced and services offered, research capacity, and a series of open-ended questions. Selected information from the survey is included in the appendices.

Table 1. Aggregate student enrollment at NAFEO member institutions, by status and gender: Fall 2005

	Undergraduate enrollment	Graduate enrollment	First professional enrollment	Total enrollment
Full-time	265,884	12,223	6,243	284,350
Part-time	107,919	17,263	629	125,811
Male	145,916	8,656	2,767	157,339
Female	227,632	20,830	4,105	252,567

N=107
Source: National Center of Education Statistics (NCES), Integrated Postsecondary Education Data System (IPEDS)

Table 2. Aggregate student enrollment at NAFEO member institutions, by level and race/ethnicity: Fall 2005

Race and ethnicity	Undergraduate enrollment		Graduate enrollment		First professional enrollment	
	Frequency	Percentage distribution	Frequency	Percentage distribution	Frequency	Percentage distribution
Total	373,548	100.0	29,486	100.0	6,872	100.0
Black, non-Hispanic	264,381	70.8	21,933	74.4	4,624	67.3
White, non-Hispanic	54,358	14.6	5,082	17.2	851	12.4
Asian or Pacific Islander	8,325	2.2	495	1.7	557	8.1
American Indian/Alaskan Native	998	0.3	74	0.3	27	0.4
Latino/Hispanic	31,571	8.5	371	1.3	353	5.1
Non-residential alien	7,730	2.1	1,152	3.9	246	3.6
Unknown	6,188	1.7	379	1.3	214	3.1

N=107
Source: NCES, IPEDS

Table 3. Aggregate faculty at NAFEO member institutions, by race and ethnicity: Fall 2005

Race and ethnicity	Number of faculty	Percentage distribution
All faculty	25,449	100
Black, non-Hispanic	13,350	52.5
White, non-Hispanic	8,365	32.9
Asian or Pacific Islander	1,895	7.4
American Indian/Alaskan Native	76	0.3
Latino/Hispanic	631	2.5
Non-residential alien	444	1.7
Unknown	688	2.7

N=107
Source: NCES, IPEDS

Majors and Degrees

Accounting – Anthropology

Table 4. Majors and degrees offered at NAFEO member institutions, Fall 2006

Institution	Accounting	African-American Studies	Agriculture	Anatomy	Animal Science	Anthropology
Alabama State University	B.S., M.S.					
Albany State University	B.S.					
Alcorn State University	B.S.		M.S.			
Allen University						
Arkansas Baptist College						
Benedict College	B.S.					
Bennett College	B.A.					
Bethune-Cookman University	B.S.					
Bishop State Community College	B.A.					
Bluefield State College	B.S.					
Bowie State University						
Central State University	B.A.					
Charles R. Drew University of Medicine & Science						
Cheyney University of Pennsylvania	Other					
Chicago State University		B.A.				B.A.
Claflin University		B.A.				
Clark Atlanta University	B.A., M.A.	M.A., Ph.D.				
Clinton Junior College						
Coahoma Community College	A.A.					
Concordia College						
Coppin State University						
Dillard University	B.A.	B.A.				
Edward Waters College						
Elizabeth City State University	B.S.					
Fayetteville State University	B.S.					
Fisk University						
Florida A&M University						
Florida Memorial University	B.A.					
Fort Valley State University	A.S., B.A.				M.S., Other	
Gadsden State Community College			A.S.			
Grambling State University	B.S.					
Hampton University	B.S.					M.A.
Harold Washington College (CCC)						
Harry Truman College (CCC)	A.AS.					
H. Councill Trenholm State Tech. College						
Hinds Community College - Utica Campus	A.A.		A.S.			
Howard University	B.A.	B.A.		B.S., M.S., Ph.D.		B.A., M.A.
Hutson-Tillotson University						
Jarvis Christian College						
J.F. Drake State Tech. College	A.A.					
Johnson C. Smith University	B.A.	B.A.				
Kennedy-King College (CCC)	A.A.	A.A.				
Kentucky State University	Other					
Lane College						
Langston University	B.A.		B.S.	B.S.		
Lawson State Community College	A.S.					
LeMoyne-Owen College						
Lewis College Of Business	A.A.					
Lincoln University (MO)	B.S.		B.S.			
Lincoln University (PA)	B.A., B.S.				B.A., B.S.	
Livingstone College	B.A.					
Malcolm X College (CCC)						
Martin University	B.A.					
Medgar Evers College (CUNY)	B.A.					
Miles College						
Mississippi Valley State University	B.S.					
Morehouse College		B.A.				
Morgan State University	B.S., Ph.D.	M.A.				B.S., M.S.
New York City College Of Technology (CUNY)	A.A.	A.A.				
Norfolk State University	B.A.					
North Carolina A&T State University	B.S.		B.S., M.S.	B.S.		
North Carolina Central University						
Oakwood College						
Olive-Harvey College (CCC)	A.AS.	A.A.				
Paine College	B.S.					
Paul Quinn College	B.A.					
Philander Smith College	B.A.					
Prairie View A&M University	B.A.		B.S.			
Richard Daley College (CCC)	A.AS.					
Roxbury Community College	A.A.		B.S.			
Saint Paul's College						
Savannah State University						
Selma University						
Shaw University	B.A.					A.A.
Shelton State Community College						
South Carolina State University	B.A.					
Southern University and A&M College	B.S.					B.A.
Southern University at New Orleans	B.S.	B.A.				
Southern University-Shreveport Bossier Campus	A.A.					
Southwestern Christian College	A.A., A.S.					
Spelman College						B.A.
Stillman College						
Talladega College	B.A.	B.A.				
Tennessee State University	B.A.	B.A.	B.S., M.S.			
Texas College						
Texas Southern University	B.A.					
Tougaloo College						
Tuskegee University			B.S., M.S.			
University of the District of Columbia	B.A.					B.S.
University of Maryland-Eastern Shore	B.S.	B.A.	B.S., M.S., Ph.D.			
University of the Virgin Islands	A.A., B.A.					
Virginia State University	B.A.		B.S.			

Institution	Accounting	African-American Studies	Agriculture	Anatomy	Animal Science	Anthropology
Virginia Union University	B.A.					
Voorhees College						
West Virginia State University	A.A.					
Wilberforce University	B.A.					
Winston-Salem State University	B.S.	B.A.				
Xavier University of Louisiana	B.S.					
York College (CUNY)	B.A.	B.A.				

Majors and Degrees

Architecture – Business Administration

Institution	Architecture	Art	Biochemistry	Biology	Botany	Business Administration
Alabama State University	B.A.		B.S., M.S.		B.S.	B.S.
Albany State University	B.A.		B.S.		Other	
Alcorn State University			B.A., M.S.		Other	
Allen University				B.S.		B.S.	B.S.
Arkansas Baptist College						A.A., B.A.
Benedict College	B.A.		B.S.		B.S.	
Bennett College				B.S.		B.A.
Bethune-Cookman University			B.S.		B.S.	B.S.
Bishop State Community College						
Bluefield State College					B.S.	
Bowie State University		B.A.		B.S.		
Central State University				B.S.		
Charles R. Drew University of Medicine & Science						
Cheyney University of Pennsylvania	B.A.	B.A.	B.A., Other		B.S.	
Chicago State University		B.A.		B.S.		B.A.
Claflin University		B.A.	B.S.	B.S.		B.A.
Clark Atlanta University	B.A.		B.S., M.S., Ph.D.		B.A., M.A.	
Clinton Junior College						A.A.
Coahoma Community College				A.S.		A.A.
Concordia College						B.A.
Coppin State University				B.S.		
Dillard University	B.A.		B.S.		B.A.	
Edward Waters College				B.S.		B.A.
Elizabeth City State University	B.A.		B.S., M.S.		B.S.	
Fayetteville State University	B.S.		B.S., M.S.		B.S., M.S.	B.S.
Fisk University		B.A.		B.S., M.S.		B.A.
Florida A&M University				B.S.		
Florida Memorial University						B.A., M.A.
Fort Valley State University			B.S.		A.S., B.A.	
Gadsden State Community College		A.A.		A.S.		A.A.
Grambling State University	B.A.		B.S.			
Hampton University			B.S., M.S.		B.S., Other	
Harold Washington College (CCC)	A.AS.	A.AS.		A.AS.		A.AS.
Harry Truman College (CCC)		A.A.		A.S., A.AS.		A.A.
H. Councill Trenholm State Tech. College						
Hinds Community College - Utica Campus		A.A.		A.S.		A.A.
Howard University				B.S., M.S., Ph.D.		
Hutson-Tillotsonon University				B.S.		
Jarvis Christian College			B.S.		B.S.	B.S.
J.F. Drake State Tech. College						
Johnson C. Smith University		B.A.		B.S.		
Kennedy-King College (CCC)		A.A.		A.S.		A.A.
Kentucky State University	B.A.		B.S.		B.A., M.A.	
Lane College				B.S.		B.A.
Langston University			B.S.			
Lawson State Community College		A.A.		A.S.		A.A.
LeMoyne-Owen College	B.A.		B.S.		B.A.	
Lewis College Of Business						A.S.
Lincoln University (MO)	B.S.		B.S.		B.S., Other	
Lincoln University (PA)			B.A., B.S.		B.A., B.S.	
Livingstone College			B.S.		B.S.	
Malcolm X College (CCC)				A.S., A.G.S.		A.A.
Martin University					B.S.	B.A.
Medgar Evers College (CUNY)						
Miles College						B.A.
Mississippi Valley State University	B.A.		B.S.		B.S., M.S.	
Morehouse College				B.S.		B.A.
Morgan State University			B.S., M.S.		B.A., M.A., Ph.D.	
New York City College Of Technology (CUNY)	A.A., B.A.	A.A.		A.S.		
Norfolk State University		B.A., M.A.		B.A.		B.A.
North Carolina A&T State University			B.S., M.S.		B.S.	B.S.
North Carolina Central University		B.A.		B.S., M.S.		
Oakwood College				B.S.		
Olive-Harvey College (CCC)		A.A., A.OS		A.S.		
Paine College			B.S.		B.S.	
Paul Quinn College				B.S.		B.A.
Philander Smith College				B.S.		
Prairie View A&M University	B.A.			B.S.		
Richard Daley College (CCC)		A.A.				A.A.
Roxbury Community College	B.A.			B.S.		
Saint Paul's College				B.S.		B.A.
Savannah State University			B.S.		M.S.	
Selma University				B.S.		B.A.
Shaw University				B.S.		B.A.
Shelton State Community College		A.A.		A.S.		A.A.
South Carolina State University		B.A.		B.S.		B.A.
Southern University and A&M College			B.S., M.S.		Other	
Southern University at New Orleans	B.A.		B.S	B.S.	B.S.	B.A.
Southern University-Shreveport Bossier Campus				A.S.		

67

Institution	Architecture	Art	Biochemistry	Biology	Botany	Business Administration
Southwestern Christian College			A.A., A.S.		A.A., A.S.	
Spelman College		B.A.	B.A.	B.A.		
Stillman College		B.A.		B.S.		B.A.
Talladega College	B.A.		B.A.		B.A.	
Tennessee State University		B.A.		B.S., M.S.	B.S.	
Texas College		B.A.		B.S.	B.S.	
Texas Southern University		B.A., M.A.		B.S., M.S.		B.A.
Tougaloo College		B.A.		B.S.		
Tuskegee University	B.A.	B.A.			B.S., M.S.	
University of the District of Columbia	B.A.					
University of Maryland-Eastern Shore	B.A.		B.S.		B.S.	B.S.
University of the Virgin Islands			B.A., B.S.		B.A., Other	
Virginia State University		B.A.		B.S., M.S.	B.S.	
Virginia Union University						
Voorhees College				B.S.		
West Virginia State University		B.A.		B.S.		
Wilberforce University				B.A.		
Winston-Salem State University	B.A.		B.S.		B.S., Other	
Xavier University of Louisiana		B.A.	B.S.	B.S.		B.S.
York College (CUNY)		B.A.		B.S.		B.S.

Majors and Degrees

Business Education – Drama

Institution	Business Education	Chemistry	Communications	Computer Science	Criminal Justice	Drafting	Drama
Alabama State University	B.S.	B.A.	B.S.	B.S.		B.A.	B.A.
Albany State University	B.S.		B.S.	B.S., M.A.		B.A.	B.A.
Alcorn State University	B.S.	B.A.	B.S., M.S.	B.S.			
Allen University	B.S.						
Arkansas Baptist College					B.A.		
Benedict College	B.S.		B.S.	B.S.			
Bennett College		B.S.		B.S.			
Bethune-Cookman University	B.S.	B.A.	B.S.	B.S.		B.A.	B.A.
Bishop State Community College				B.S.	B.A.		
Bluefield State College			B.S.	B.S.			
Bowie State University		B.S.	B.A.	B.S.	B.A.		
Central State University							
Charles R. Drew University of Medicine & Science							
Cheyney University of Pennsylvania	B.A.	B.A.	B.A.			B.A.	B.A.
Chicago State University		B.S.	B.A.		B.A.		B.A.
Claflin University		B.S.	B.A.	B.S.			
Clark Atlanta University	B.S., M.S., Ph.D.	B.A.	B.S., M.S.	B.A., M.A.			
Clinton Junior College							
Coahoma Community College		A.S.		A.S.	A.A.		
Concordia College							
Coppin State University		B.S.		B.A.	B.A.		
Dillard University	B.S.	B.A.	B.S.				
Edward Waters College			B.A.	B.S.	B.A.		
Elizabeth City State University	B.S.	B.A.	B.S.	B.S.			
Fayetteville State University	B.A, B.S.	B.A.	B.S.	B.S., M.S.			
Fisk University		B.S.					
Florida A&M University		B.S.		B.S.			
Florida Memorial University		B.S., M.S.	B.A.	B.S.	B.A.		
Fort Valley State University	B.S.	B.A.	B.S.	B.A.			
Gadsden State Community College		A.S.		A.S.	A.A.		
Grambling State University	B.S.	B.A, M.A.	B.S.	A.S., B.S., M.S	B.S.	B.S.	B.S.
Hampton University	B.S.		B.S., M.S.	B.S.			
Harold Washington College (CCC)			A.AS.				
Harry Truman College (CCC)		A.S.		A.AS.	A.AS.		
H. Council Trenholm State Tech. College							
Hinds Community College - Utica Campus				A.S.			
Howard University		B.S. M.S., Ph.D.	B.A., M.A.	B.S., M.S., Ph.D.			
Hutson-Tillotsonon University		B.S.			B.A.		
Jarvis Christian College	B.S.		B.S.	B.S.			
J.F. Drake State Tech. College							
Johnson C. Smith University		B.S.	B.A.	B.S.			
Kennedy-King College (CCC)		A.S.		A.S.			A.A.
Kentucky State University	B.S.		B.S., M.S.	B.A.			
Lane College		B.S.	B.A.	B.S.	B.A.		
Langston University	B.S.		B.S.	A.S.	A.S.	B.A.	B.A.
Lawson State Community College				A.S.	A.A.		
LeMoyne-Owen College	B.S.		B.S.	B.A.			
Lewis College Of Business							
Lincoln University (MO)	B.S.		B.S., Other	B.S.	Other		
Lincoln University (PA)	B.A., B.S.	B.A., B.S.	B.A., B.S.	B.A., B.S.			
Livingstone College	B.S.		B.S.				
Malcolm X College (CCC)		A.S.	A.G.S.	A.S.			A.A.
Martin University		B.S.			B.A.		
Medgar Evers College (CUNY)				A.S., B.S.			
Miles College			B.A.		B.A.		
Mississippi Valley State University	B.S.	B.A.	B.S.	B.S., M.S.			
Morehouse College		B.S.	B.A.	B.S.			
Morgan State University	B.S., M.S.	B.A, B.S., M.S.	B.S., M.S.	Other	Other	Other	Other
New York City College Of Technology (CUNY)		A.S.	B.A.	B.S.			
Norfolk State University		B.S.	B.A., M.A.	B.S., M.S.	B.A., M.A.		
North Carolina A&T State University	B.S., M.S.	B.S., M.S.	B.S., M.S.	B.S.			
North Carolina Central University		B.S., M.S.	B.A.	B.S.	B.A., M.A.		B.A.
Oakwood College		B.S.	B.A.	B.S.			
Olive-Harvey College (CCC)		A.S.	A.O.S.	A.AS.			
Paine College	B.S.	B.A.	B.S.	B.A.		B.A.	B.A.
Paul Quinn College			B.A.	B.S.	B.A.		
Philander Smith College		B.S.		B.S.			
Prairie View A&M University		B.S.	B.A.	B.S.	B.A.		B.A.
Richard Daley College (CCC)				A.AS.	A.AS.		A.A.
Roxbury Community College		B.S.	B.A.	A.S.	A.A.		A.A.
Saint Paul's College					B.A.	B.A.	
Savannah State University	B.S.	B.A.	B.S.	B.A.			
Selma University				A.S.			
Shaw University		B.S.	B.A.	B.S.	B.A.		B.A.
Shelton State Community College		A.S.	A.A.	A.S.	A.A.		A.A.
South Carolina State University		B.S.		B.S.			B.S.
Southern University and A&M College	B.S., M.S.		B.S., M.S.	A.S., B.S., M.S			
Southern University at New Orleans	B.S.			B.S., M.A.	B.A., M.A.		
Southern University-Shreveport Bossier Campus		A.S.		A.S.	A.A.		
Southwestern Christian College			A.A., A.S.				
Spelman College		B.S.		B.S.			B.A.
Stillman College				B.S.			
Talladega College	B.A.		B.A.				
Tennessee State University		B.S., M.S.	B.A.	B.S., M.S., Ph.D.			B.A.

Institution	Business Education	Chemistry	Communications	Computer Science	Criminal Justice	Drafting	Drama
Texas College				B.S.			
Texas Southern University		B.S., M.S., Ph.D.		B.S., M.S.			
Tougaloo College		B.S.	B.A.	B.S.			
Tuskegee University				B.S.			
University of the District of Columbia	B.S.	B.S.	B.S.	A.S.		B.A.	B.A.
University of Maryland-Eastern Shore	B.S.		B.S., M.S.	B.S., M.S.			
University of the Virgin Islands	B.A., B.S.		A.S., B.S.				
Virginia State University		B.S.	B.A.	B.S.	B.A., M.A.		
Virginia Union University	B.A.			B.S.			
Voorhees College			B.A.	B.S.			
West Virginia State University		B.S.	A.A., B.A	A.S.	A.A.		
Wilberforce University			B.A.	B.S.			
Winston-Salem State University	B.S.		B.S., M.S., Other				
Xavier University of Louisiana		B.S.	B.A.	B.S.			
York College (CUNY)		B.A., B.S.	B.A.	B.S.			

Majors and Degrees

Earth Science - Education (Secondary)

Institution	Earth Science	Ecology	Economics	Education (Early Childhood)	Education (Elementary)	Education (Secondary)
Alabama State University				B.S., Other	B.S., Other	B.S., Other
Albany State University				B.S., Other		
Alcorn State University			B.A.		B.S., Other	Other
Allen University						
Benedict College			B.S.	B.S.	B.S.	
Bennett College				B.A.	B.A.	B.A.
Bethune-Cookman University					B.S.	B.S.
Bishop State Community College				B.A.		
Bluefield State College					B.S.	
Bowie State University			B.A.			
Central State University	B.S.		B.A.	B.A.	B.A.	B.A.
Cheyney University of Pennsylvania			B.A.	Other	Other	Other
Chicago State University			B.A.	B.A.	B.A.	B.A.
Claflin University				B.A.	B.A.	
Clark Atlanta University			B.A., M.A.	B.A.		M.A.
Clinton Junior College				A.A.		
Coahoma Community College				A.A.	A.A.	A.A.
Concordia College				B.A.	B.A.	B.A.
Coppin State University				B.A.	B.A.	
Dillard University			B.A.		B.A.	B.A.
Edward Waters College					B.A.	
Elizabeth City State University				B.S.	Other	B.S.
Fayetteville State University					B.S., M.S.	B.S., M.S.
Fisk University						
Florida A&M University			B.A.			
Florida Memorial University					B.A.	
Fort Valley State University			B.A.			M.S., Other
Gadsden State Community College				A.A.	A.A.	A.A.
Grambling State University			B.S.	B.S.	B.S., M.S.	
Hampton University				M.A.	M.A.	M.A.
Harold Washington College (CCC)						
Hinds Community College – Utica Campus						
Howard University		B.S.	B.A., M.A., Ph.D.		5yr, M.Ed.	M.A., M.Ed.
Hutson-Tillotson University						
Jarvis Christian College				B.S.	B.S.	B.S.
Johnson C. Smith University			B.A.		B.A.	
Kennedy-King College (CCC)					A.A.	A.A.
Kentucky State University				B.A.	B.A.	
Lane College						
Langston University			B.A.	B.S.	B.S., M.S.	B.A.
Lawson State Community College				A.A.	A.A.	
LeMoyne-Owen College				B.A.		
Lincoln University (MO)			B.A., B.S.	Other	B.S., Other	B.S. Other
Lincoln University (PA)				B.A., B.S., M.A.	B.A., B.S., M.A.	B.A., B.S., M.A.
Livingstone College				B.A.	B.A.	B.A.
Malcolm X College (CCC)						
Martin University						
Miles College				B.A.	B.A.	B.A.
Mississippi Valley State University				B.S.	B.S., M.S.	B.S.
Morehouse College			B.S.			
Morgan State University			B.A., B.S., M.A.		B.S., M.S.	M.S., Other
Morris College				B.A.	B.A.	
New York City College Of Technology (CUNY)						
Norfolk State University				B.A., M.A.	B.A., M.A.	B.A., M.A.
North Carolina A&T State University			B.S.		B.S., M.A.	B.S., M.S.
North Carolina Central University	B.S., M.S.			B.A., M.A.	B.A., M.A.	
Oakwood College				B.A.	B.A.	B.A.
Olive-Harvey College (CCC)	A.S.			A.A.S.		
Paine College					B.S.	B.S.
Paul Quinn College					B.A.	B.A.
Philander Smith College				B.A.	B.A.	B.A.
Prairie View A&M University						B.A.
Richard Daley College (CCC)					A.A.	
Roxbury Community College				A.A.		
Saint Paul's College						
Savannah State University						
Selma University						
Shaw University				B.A., M.A.	B.A.	B.A.
Shelton State Community College			A.A.			
South Carolina State University				B.A.	B.A.	B.A.
Southern University and A&M College			B.S.	B.S.	B.S.	B.S.
Southern University at New Orleans				B.S.	B.S.	
Southwestern Christian College					A.A., A.S.	A.A., A.S.
Spelman College			B.A.	B.A.	B.A.	B.A.
Stillman College				B.A.	B.A.	B.A.
Talladega College			B.A.			B.A.
Tennessee State University				B.A., M.A.	B.A., M.A.	B.A., M.A.
Texas College				A.A.		
Texas Southern University			B.A.	B.A.		
Tougaloo College			B.A.			B.A.
Tuskegee University			B.A.			
University of the District of Columbia	B.S.		B.A.	B.A.	B.A.	
University of Maryland-Eastern Shore						
University of the Virgin Islands				A.A., B.A.	A.A., M.A.	
Virginia State University			B.A., M.A.		B.A.	B.A.
Virginia Union University					B.A.	B.A.
Voorhees College						
West Virginia State University			B.A.	B.A.		
Wilberforce University						
Winston-Salem State University			B.S.	B.S.	B.S., Other	B.S.
Xavier University of LA				B.A.	B.A.	B.A.
York College (CUNY)						

Majors and Degrees

Education (Special) - French

Institution	Education (Special)	English	Electronics	Engineering	Finance	French
Alabama State University	B.S., Other	B.A.			B.S.	
Albany State University	B.S., Other	B.A., Other				
Alcorn State University		B.A.				
Allen University		B.S.				
Benedict College		B.A.		B.S.		
Bennett College	B.A.					
Bethune-Cookman University	B.S.	B.A.		B.A.		
Bishop State Community College		B.A.				
Bluefield State College		B.A.				
Bowie State University		B.A.			B.A.	
Central State University		B.A.		B.S.	B.A.	
Cheyney University of Pennsylvania	M.S., Other	B.A.				Other
Chicago State University	B.A.	B.A.				
Claflin University		B.A.				
Clark Atlanta University	B.A., M.A.	B.A., M.A., Ph.D.				B.A., M.A.
Clinton Junior College						
Coahoma Community College						
Concordia College	B.A.					
Coppin State University	B.A.	B.A.				
Dillard University	B.A.	B.A.			B.A.	
Edward Waters College						
Elizabeth City State University	Other	B.A.		B.S.		
Fayetteville State University	M.S.	B.A., M.A.			B.S.	
Fisk University	B.A.	B.A.		B.S.	B.A.	
Florida A&M University						
Florida Memorial University		B.A.		B.S.	B.A.	
Fort Valley State University		B.A.				
Gadsden State Community College	A.A.	A.A.				
Grambling State University	B.S., M.S., Ph.D.	B.A.	M.A.	M.A.		B.A.
Hampton University	M.A.	M.A.	M.A.	M.A.		
Harold Washington College (CCC)		A.A.S.				
Hinds Community College – Utica Campus			A.S.		A.A.	
Howard University	M.A., M.Ed.	B.A., M.A., Ph.D.		B.S., M.S., Ph.D.	B.A.	B.A.
Hutson-Tillotson University		B.A.				
Jarvis Christian College	B.S.	B.A.				
Johnson C. Smith University		B.A.		B.S.	B.A.	B.A.
Kennedy-King College (CCC)		A.A.				
Kentucky State University	M.A.	B.A.	A.S.			
Lane College		B.A.		B.S.		B.A.
Langston University	B.S.	B.A.	A.S.		B.A.	
Lawson State Community College		A.A.				
LeMoyne-Owen College	B.A.	B.A.				
Lincoln University (MO)	B.S.	B.A.		A.S.		
Lincoln University (PA)	B.A., B.S.	B.A., B.S.		B.A., B.S.	B.A., B.S., M.S.	B.A., B.S.
Livingstone College		B.A.				
Malcolm X College (CCC)		A.A.				
Martin University						
Miles College						
Mississippi Valley State University	M.S.	B.A.				
Morehouse College		B.A.		B.S.		
Morgan State University		B.A., M.A., Ph.D.		B.S., M.S., Ph.D.	B.S.	Other
Morris College		B.A.				
New York City College Of Technology (CUNY)		A.A.		A.S.		
Norfolk State University	B.A., M.A.	B.A.		B.S., M.S.		
North Carolina A&T State University	B.S.	B.S., M.S.	B.S., M.S.	B.S., M.S., Ph.D.	B.S.	
North Carolina Central University	B.A., M.A.	B.A., M.A.				
Oakwood College		B.A.				
Olive-Harvey College (CCC)						
Paine College		B.A.				

Institution	Education (Special)	English	Electronics	Engineering	Finance	French
Paul Quinn College				B.S.		
Philander Smith College		B.A.				
Prairie View A&M University				B.S., M.S.	B.A.	
Richard Daley College (CCC)				A.S.		
Roxbury Community College						
Saint Paul's College						
Savannah State University		B.A.		B.S.		
Selma University		A.A.				
Shaw University	B.A.	B.A.				
Shelton State Community College		A.A.		A.A.		
South Carolina State University	B.A.	B.A.		B.A.		B.A.
Southern University and A&M College	B.S., Ph.D., Other	B.A.		B.S., M.S.	B.S.	B.A.
Southern University at New Orleans		B.A.				
Southwestern Christian College						
Spelman College		B.A.		B.A.		B.A.
Stillman College						
Talladega College		B.A.			B.A.	
Tennessee State University	B.A., M.A.	B.A., M.A.		B.S., M.S.	B.A.	
Texas College		B.A.				
Texas Southern University		B.A., M.A.		B.S., M.S.	B.A.	B.A.
Tougaloo College		B.A.				
Tuskegee University				B.S.		
University of the District of Columbia	B.S., M.A.	B.A., M.A.	A.S.	B.S.	B.A.	B.A.
University of Maryland-Eastern Shore	B.S., M.S.	B.A.		B.S.		
University of the Virgin Islands		B.A.				
Virginia State University		B.A.		B.S.		
Virginia Union University	B.A.	B.A.			B.A.	
Voorhees College		B.A.				
West Virginia State University		B.A.				
Wilberforce University		B.A.		B.S.		
Winston-Salem State University	B.S., Other	B.A.			B.S.	
Xavier University of LA	B.A.	B.A.				B.A.
York College (CUNY)		B.A.				B.A.

Majors and Degrees

Geography – Horticulture

Institution	Geography	German	Gerontology	Health Science	History	Home Economics	Horticulture
Alabama State University					B.A.		
Albany State University					B.A.		
Alcorn State University				B.S.	B.A.		
Allen University							
Benedict College					B.A.		
Bennett College							
Bethune-Cookman University				B.S.	B.A.		
Bishop State Community College					B.A.		
Bluefield State College	B.A.				B.A.		
Bowie State University					B.A.		
Central State University	B.A.		B.A.		B.A.		
Cheyney University of Pennsylvania						Other	
Chicago State University				B.S.			
Claflin University					B.A.		
Clark Atlanta University					B.A., M.A., Ph.D.		
Clinton Junior College							
Coahoma Community College							
Concordia College							
Coppin State University					B.A.		
Dillard University				B.S.	B.A.		
Edward Waters College							
Elizabeth City State University					B.A.		
Fayetteville State University	B.A.				B.A.		
Fisk University					B.A.		
Florida A&M University							
Florida Memorial University							
Fort Valley State University					B.A.	Other	Other
Gadsden State Community College				A.S.	A.A.		
Grambling State University					B.A.		
Hampton University					M.A.		
Harold Washington College (CCC)							
Hinds Community College – Utica Campus	A.S.			A.S.	A.A.		
Howard University		B.A.			B.A., Ph.D.		
Hutson-Tillotson University				A.S.			
Jarvis Christian College					B.S.		
Johnson C. Smith University							
Kennedy-King College (CCC)				A.S.	A.A.		
Kentucky State University					Other		
Lane College					B.A.		
Langston University			B.A.		B.A.	B.S.	A.A.
Lawson State Community College					A.A.		
LeMoyne-Owen College					B.A.		
Lincoln University (MO)					B.A., B.S., M.A.		
Lincoln University (PA)				B.A., B.S.	B.A., B.S.		
Livingstone College					B.A.		
Malcolm X College (CCC)					A.A.		
Martin University							
Miles College							
Mississippi Valley State University					B.S.		
Morehouse College				B.S.	B.A.		
Morgan State University	Other	Other		B.S.	B.A., M.A., Ph.D.	B.S.	
Morris College				B.S.	B.A.		
New York City College Of Technology (CUNY)							
Norfolk State University				B.S.	B.A.		
North Carolina A&T State University					B.S., M.S.	B.S., M.S.	
North Carolina Central University				B.S.	B.A., M.A.		
Oakwood College				B.S.	B.A.		
Olive-Harvey College (CCC)							
Paine College							
Paul Quinn College							
Philander Smith College							
Prairie View A&M University							
Richard Daley College (CCC)							
Roxbury Community College							
Saint Paul's College					B.A.		
Savannah State University					B.A.		
Selma University					A.A.		
Shaw University							
Shelton State Community College	A.A.			A.S.	A.A.	A.A.	
South Carolina State University				B.S.	B.A.		
Southern University and A&M College				M.S.	B.A.		
Southern University at New Orleans					B.A.		
Southwestern Christian College					A.A., A.S.		
Spelman College				B.S.	B.A.		
Stillman College					B.A.		
Talladega College							
Tennessee State University				B.S.	B.A.		
Texas College					B.A.		
Texas Southern University	B.S.			B.S., M.S.	B.A.		
Tougaloo College					B.A.		
Tuskegee University				B.S.	B.A.		B.S.
University of the District of Columbia				A.S., B.S.	B.A.		
University of Maryland-Eastern Shore					B.A.	B.S.	
University of the Virgin Islands							
Virginia State University					B.A.		
Virginia Union University							
Voorhees College				B.S.			
West Virginia State University			A.S.	A.S., B.S.	B.A.		
Wilberforce University				B.S.			
Winston-Salem State University			B.A.		B.A.		
Xavier University of LA					B.A.		
York College (CUNY)				B.S.	B.A.		

Majors and Degrees

Industrial Administration - Management

Institution	Industrial Administration	International Studies	Journalism	Law	Library Science	Management
Alabama A&M University						
Alabama State University						B.S.
Albany State University			B.A.			B.S.
Alcorn State University						
Allen University						
Benedict College						
Bennett College			B.A.			
Bethune-Cookman University			B.A.			B.S.
Bishop State Community College						
Bluefield State College						
Bowie State University						
Central State University			B.A.			B.A.
Cheyney University of Pennsylvania						
Chicago State University						B.A.
Clark Atlanta University						
Claflin University						B.A.
Coahoma Community College						
Coppin State University						B.A.
Dillard University						B.A.
Edward Waters College						
Elizabeth City State University						
Fayetteville State University						
Fisk University						
Florida Memorial University						B.A.
Fort Valley State University						A.S., B.A.
Gadsden State Community College						
Grambling State University		B.S.				B.S.
Harry Truman College (CCC)			A.A.			
Hampton University			B.S.			B.S.
Harold Washington College (CCC)						
Hinds Community College – Utica Campus		A.A.				
Howard University			B.A.	B.A., J.D.		B.A.
Hutson-Tillotson University						
Jarvis Christian College						
J.F. Drake State Tech. College						
Johnson C. Smith University						B.A.
Kennedy-King College (CCC)			A.A.			A.AS.
Kentucky State University			B.A.			Other
Lane College						
Langston University			B.A.			B.A.
Lawson State Community College						
LeMoyne-Owen College						
Lewis College Business						A.A.
Lincoln University (MO)			B.A., B.S.			
Lincoln University (PA)			B.A., B.S.			
Livingstone College						
Malcolm X College (CCC)						
Medgar Evers College (CUNY)						
Miles College			B.A.			B.A.
Mississippi Valley State University						
Morehouse College						
Morehouse School of Medicine						
Morgan State University		M.A.				B.S.
Morris College			B.A.			
New York City College Of Technology (CUNY)				A.A., B.A.		
North Carolina A&T State University			B.S.			B.S., M.S.
North Carolina Central University					M.A.	
Oakwood College						
Olive-Harvey College (CCC)						
Paine College			B.A.			B.S.
Paul Quinn College						
Philander Smith College						
Prairie View A&M University			A.A.			A.AS.
Richard Daley College (CCC)						
Roxbury Community College						
Saint Paul's College						
Savannah State University						B.S.
Selma University						
Shaw University			B.A.			
Shelton State Community College						
South Carolina State University						
Southern University and A&M College						B.S.
Southern University at New Orleans						B.S., M.S.
Southwestern Christian College			A.A., A.S.			
Spelman College		B.A.				
Talladega College						
Tennesse State University						
Texas Southern University						
Tougaloo College						
Tuskegee University			B.A.			B.A.
University of the District of Columbia						B.A.
University of Maryland-Eastern Shore						
University of the Virgin Islands						A.A.
Virginia State University						
Virginia Union University						B.A.
Virginia University of Lynchburg						
Voorhees College						
West Virginia State University						
Winston-Salem State University						B.S.
Xavier University of Louisiana						
York College (CUNY)						

Majors and Degrees

Marketing – Modern Languages

Institution	Marketing	Mathematics	Medical Science	Medical Technology	Microbiology	Modern Languages
Alabama A&M University		B.S.				
Alabama State University	B.S.	B.S., M.S.			Ph.D.	
Albany State University	B.S.	B.A.				
Alcorn State University		B.S.				
Allen University		B.S.				
Benedict College		B.S.				
Bennett College		B.S.				
Bethune-Cookman University	B.S.	B.S.				
Bishop State Community College						
Bluefield State College						
Bowie State University		B.S.				B.A.
Central State University	B.A.	B.S.				B.A.
Cheyney University of Pennsylvania		B.A.		B.S.		
Chicago State University	B.A.					
Clark Atlanta University		B.S., M.S.				
Claflin University	B.A.	B.S.				
Coahoma Community College		A.S.				
Coppin State University						
Dillard University	B.A.					
Edward Waters College		B.S.				
Elizabeth City State University		B.S., M.S.				
Fayetteville State University	B.S.	B.S., M.S.				
Fisk University		B.S.				
Florida Memorial University	B.A.	B.S.				
Fort Valley State University	A.S., B.A.	B.S.				
Gadsden State Community College	A.A.	A.S.				
Grambling State University	B.S.	B.S.				
Harry Truman College (CCC)		A.S.				A.A.
Hampton University	B.S.	B.S., M.S.	M.S.			
Harold Washington College (CCC)		A.S.				
Hinds Community College – Utica Campus	A.A.			A.S.		
Howard University	B.A.	B.S., M.S., Ph.D.			B.S., M.S., Ph.D.	B.A., M.A.
Hutson-Tillotson University		B.A.				
Jarvis Christian College		B.S.				
J.F. Drake State Tech. College						
Johnson C. Smith University	B.A.	B.S.				
Kennedy-King College (CCC)	A.AS.	A.S.				
Kentucky State University	Other	B.S.				
Lane College		B.S.				
Langston University		B.S.				
Lawson State Community College		A.S.				
LeMoyne-Owen College		B.S.				
Lewis College Business	A.A.					
Lincoln University (MO)	B.S.	B.A., B.S.		B.S.		
Lincoln University (PA)		B.A., B.S., M.S.				
Livingstone College		B.S.				
Malcolm X College (CCC)		A.S., A.GS.				
Medgar Evers College (CUNY)		B.S.				
Miles College		B.S.				
Mississippi Valley State University		B.S.				
Morehouse College		B.S.				B.A.
Morehouse School of Medicine						
Morgan State University	B.S.	B.A., M.A., Other		B.S.		
Morris College		B.S.				
New York City College Of Technology (CUNY)	A.A.	A.S.				
North Carolina A&T State University	B.S.	B.S., M.S.				
North Carolina Central University		B.S.				B.A.
Oakwood College		B.S.				B.A.
Olive-Harvey College (CCC)		A.S., A.O.S				
Paine College	B.S.	B.S.				
Paul Quinn College		B.S.				
Philander Smith College		B.S.				
Prairie View A&M University	B.A.	B.S.				
Richard Daley College (CCC)	A.AS.					A.A.
Roxbury Community College		B.S.				
Saint Paul's College		B.S.				
Savannah State University	B.S.	B.S.				
Selma University		A.S.				
Shaw University						
Shelton State Community College						
South Carolina State University	B.A.	B.S.				
Southern University and A&M College	B.S.	B.S., M.S.				
Southern University at New Orleans		B.S.				
Southwestern Christian College		A.A., A.S.				
Spelman College		B.S.				
Talladega College	B.A.	B.A.				
Tennesse State University		B.S., M.S.				B.A.
Texas Southern University		B.S., M.S.				
Tougaloo College		B.S.				
Tuskegee University		B.S.				
University of the District of Columbia	B.A.	B.S., M.S.				
University of Maryland-Eastern Shore		B.S.				
University of the Virgin Islands		B.A., B.S., M.S.				
Virginia State University	B.A.	B.S., M.S.				
Virginia Union University	B.A.					
Virginia University of Lynchburg	B.A.					
Voorhees College		B.S.				
West Virginia State University		B.A.				B.A.
Winston-Salem State University	B.S.	B.S.				
Xavier University of Louisiana		B.S.			B.S.	
York College (CUNY)	B.A.	B.A., B.S.		B.S.		

Majors and Degrees

Music Education – Physics

Institution	Music Education	Music Performance	Nursing	Office Administration	Philosophy	Physical Therapy	Physics
Alabama A&M University							
Alabama State University	B.S., Other	M.A.		B.S.		Other	B.S.
Albany State University	Other		B.S., M.S.				
Alcorn State University		Other	A.S., B.S., M.S.				
Allen University		B.S.					B.S.
Benedict College	B.S.						
Bennett College							
Bethune-Cookman University	B.A.	B.A.	B.S.				B.S.
Bishop State Community College			B.S.				
Bluefield State College			A.S., B.S.				
Bowie State University	B.A.	B.A.	B.S.		B.A.		B.S.
Central State University							B.S.
Cheyney University of Pennsylvania							
Chicago State University	B.A.						B.S.
Clark Atlanta University		B.A.			B.A.		B.S., M.S.
Claflin University	B.A.				B.A.		
Coahoma Community College			A.S.				
Coppin State University			B.S.				
Dillard University		B.A.	Other		B.A.		B.S.
Edward Waters College					B.A.		
Elizabeth City State University	B.A.						B.S.
Fayetteville State University	B.S.		B.S.				
Fisk University	B.A., M.A.						B.S., M.S.
Florida Memorial University					B.A.		
Fort Valley State University		B.A.					
Gadsden State Community College				A.A.			B.S.
Grambling State University	Other	B.A.	B.S., M.S., Other				B.S.
Harry Truman College (CCC)			A.A.S.				A.S.
Hampton University	B.S.	B.A.	B.S.				B.S., M.S., Ph.D.
Harold Washington College (CCC)						A.S.	A.S.
Hinds Community College – Utica Campus		A.A.		A.A.			
Howard University	B.A.		B.S. M.S.		B.A., M.A.		B.S., M.S., Ph.D
Hutson-Tillotson University	B.A.	B.A.					
Jarvis Christian College	B.S.						
J.F. Drake State Tech. College			A.S.				
Johnson C. Smith University							
Kennedy-King College (CCC)		A.A.	A.A.S.		A.A.		A.S.
Kentucky State University	B.A.	B.A.	B.S.				B.S.
Lane College		B.A.					
Langston University	B.A.		B.S.			Other	
Lawson State Community College	A.A.		A.S.	A.S.			
LeMoyne-Owen College							
Lewis College Business							
Lincoln University (MO)	B.S.		B.S., Other	Other			B.S.
Lincoln University (PA)	B.A., B.S.	B.A., B.S.			B.A., B.S.		B.A., B.S.
Livingstone College	B.A.	B.A.					
Malcolm X College (CCC)			A.A.S., A.S.				A.S.
Medgar Evers College (CUNY)			B.S.				
Miles College		B.A.					
Mississippi Valley State University	B.S.	B.A.		B.S.			
Morehouse College		B.A.			B.A.		B.S.
Morehouse School of Medicine							
Morgan State University	B.A., M.A.		B.S., M.S.		B.A.		B.S.
Morris College							
New York City College Of Technology (CUNY)			A.S., B.S.				B.S.
North Carolina A&T State University	B.A.		B.S.				B.S., M.S.
North Carolina Central University		B.A.	B.S.				B.S.
Oakwood College		B.A.	B.S.				
Olive-Harvey College (CCC)			A.A.S.		A.A.		A.S.
Paine College		B.A.			B.A.		
Paul Quinn College							
Philander Smith College		B.A.		B.A.	B.A.		
Prairie View A&M University		B.A.	B.S., M.S.				B.S.
Richard Daley College (CCC)			A.A.S.				
Roxbury Community College		B.A.	A.S.				
Saint Paul's College							
Savannah State University		B.A.					
Selma University							A.S.
Shaw University							
Shelton State Community College		A.A.					A.S.
South Carolina State University	B.A.	B.A.	B.S.				B.S.
Southern University and A&M College	Other	Other	B.S., M.S., Ph.D., Other				B.S., M.S.
Southern University at New Orleans							B.S.
Southwestern Christian College	A.A., A.S.						
Spelman College		B.A.			B.A.		B.S.
Talladega College	B.A.	B.A.					
Tennesse State University	B.A., M.A.	B.A.	B.S., M.S.			B.S., Ph.D.	B.S, M.S.
Texas Southern University							B.S.
Tougaloo College		B.A.					B.S.
Tuskegee University							
University of the District of Columbia	A.A., B.A.		A.S., B.S.	B.S.			B.S.
University of Maryland-Eastern Shore	B.A.					Ph.D.	
University of the Virgin Islands	B.A.		A.S., B.S.				A.S.
Virginia State University		B.A.	B.S.				B.S.
Virginia Union University							
Virginia University of Lynchburg							
Voorhees College							
West Virginia State University		B.A.					B.A.

Institution	Music Education	Music Performance	Nursing	Office Administration	Philosophy	Physical Therapy	Physics
Winston-Salem State University	B.S.		B.S., M.S.			Other	
Xavier University of Louisiana	B.A.	B.A.			B.A.		
York College (CUNY)		B.A.	B.S.		B.A.		B.S.

85

Majors and Degrees

Physiology - Psychology

Institution	Physiology	Political Science	Pre-dentistry	Pre-medicine	Pre-optometry	Psychology
Alabama A&M University		B.A.				
Alabama State University		B.A.				B.S.
Albany State University		B.A.				B.A.
Alcorn State University		B.A.				B.S.
Allen University						
Arkansas Baptist College						
Benedict College		B.A.				B.A.
Bennett College		B.A.				B.A.
Bethune-Cookman University		B.A.				B.S.
Bishop State Community College						B.A.
Bluefield State College		B.A.		B.S.		B.A.
Central State University		B.A.				B.A.
Cheyney University of Pennsylvania		B.A.				B.A.
Chicago State University						B.A.
Claflin University						
Clark Atlanta University		B.A., M.A., Ph.D.				B.A.
Clinton Junior College						
Coahoma Community College		A.A.				A.A.
Coppin State University						B.A.
Dillard University		B.A.				B.A.
Edward Waters College		B.A.				B.A.
Elizabeth City State University		B.A.				B.S
Fayetteville State University		B.A., M.A.	B.S.	B.S.		B.S., M.A.
Fisk University		B.A.				B.A., M.A.
Florida A&M University						
Florida Memorial University		B.A.				B.A.
Fort Valley State University		B.A.				B.A.
Gadsden State Community College						A.A.
Grambling State University		B.A.				B.A.
Hampton University		B.S.				B.S.
Harold Washington College (CCC)						
Harry Truman College (CCC)	A.A.					
Hinds Community College – Utica Campus						A.A.
Howard University	Ph.D.	B.A., Ph.D.				B.A., Ph.D.
Hutson-Tillotson University		B.A.				B.A.
Jarvis Christian College						
Johnson C. Smith University						
Kennedy-King College (CCC)		A.A.				A.A.
Kentucky State University		B.A.				
Lane College						
Langston University						B.S.
Lawson State Community College		A.A.				A.A.
LeMoyne-Owen College		B.A.				
Lincoln University (MO)		B.A., B.S.				B.A., B.S.
Lincoln University (PA)		B.A., B.S.				B.A., B.S.
Livingstone College		B.A.				B.A.
Malcom X College (CCC)						A.A.
Martin University						B.A.
Medgar Evers College (CUNY)						
Miles College		B.A.				
Mississippi Valley State University		B.A.				
Morehouse College		B.A.				
Morehouse School of Medicine						
Morgan State University		B.S.				B.S., M.S., Ph.D.
Morris College		B.A.				
New York College Of Technology (CUNY)						
Norfolk State University		B.A.				B.A., M.A.
North Carolina A&T State University		B.S.				B.S.
North Carolina Central University		B.A.				B.A.
Oakwood College						B.A.
Olive-Harvey College (CCC)						
Paine College						B.A.
Paul Quinn College						
Philander Smith College		B.A.				B.A.
Prairie View A&M University		B.A.				B.A.
Richard Daley College (CCC)			A.S.	A.S.	A.S.	
Roxbury Community College						
Saint Augustine's College						
Saint Paul's College		B.A.				
Savannah State University						B.S.
Selma University		A.A.				
Shaw University						B.A.
Shorter College						
Simmons Bible College						
Sojourner Douglass College						
South Carolina State University		B.A.	B.S.		B.S.	B.A.
Southern University and A&M College		B.S.				B.S.
Southern University at New Orleans		B.A.				B.A.
Southwestern Christian College						
Spellman College						B.A.
Talladega College		B.A.				B.A.
Tennesse State University						B.A., M.A., Ph.D.
Texas College		B.A.				B.A.
Texas Southern University						B.A., M.A.
Tougaloo College						
Tuskegee University		B.A.				B.A.
University of the District of Columbia		B.S.				B.S.
University of Maryland-Eastern Shore						
University of the Virgin Islands						B.A.
Virginia State University		B.A.				B.A., M.A.
Virginia Union University		B.A.				
Virginia University of Lynchburg						

Institution	Physiology	Political Science	Pre-dentistry	Pre-medicine	Pre-optometry	Psychology
West Virginia State University		B.A.				B.A.
Wilberforce University		B.A.				B.A.
Wiley College						
Winston-Salem State University		B.A.				B.S.
Xavier University of Louisiana		B.A.				B.A.
York College (CUNY)		B.A.				B.A.

Majors and Degrees

Public Administration – Social Science

Institution	Public Administration	Radiological Technology	Religion	Russian	Secretarial Science	Social Science
Alabama A&M University						
Alabama State University	M.S.					
Albany State University	Other					
Alcorn State University						
Allen University			B.S.			B.S.
Arkansas Baptist College	A.A., B.A.		A.A., B.A.			
Benedict College			B.A.			
Bennett College						
Bethune-Cookman University			B.A.			B.A.
Bishop State Community College						
Bluefield State College		A.S., B.S.				B.A.
Central State University			B.A.			B.A.
Cheyney University of Pennsylvania	Other					B.A., Other
Chicago State University						
Claflin University			B.A.			
Clark Atlanta University	M.A.		B.A.			
Clinton Junior College			A.A.			
Coahoma Community College					A.A.	A.A.
Coppin State University						B.A.
Dillard University			B.A.			
Edward Waters College			B.A.			
Elizabeth City State University						
Fayetteville State University						
Fisk University			B.A.			
Florida A&M University						
Florida Memorial University	B.A.		B.A.			
Fort Valley State University						
Gadsden State Community College			A.A.		A.A.	
Grambling State University	M.A.					M.A.
Hampton University			B.S.			
Harold Washington College (CCC)						A.S.
Harry Truman College (CCC)						A.A.
Hinds Community College – Utica Campus						
Howard University			M.A.	B.A.		
Hutson-Tillotson University			B.A.			
Jarvis Christian College						
Johnson C. Smith University						B.A.
Kennedy-King College (CCC)						
Kentucky State University	B.A., M.A.					B.A.
Lane College			B.A.			
Langston University						
Lawson State Community College						
LeMoyne-Owen College						B.A.
Lincoln University (MO)	B.S.					M.A.
Lincoln University (PA)			B.A., B.S.			
Livingstone College						
Malcom X College (CCC)						
Martin University			B.A.			
Medgar Evers College (CUNY)	A.A., B.A.					
Miles College						B.A.
Mississippi Valley State University	B.S.					
Morehouse College			B.A.			
Morehouse School of Medicine						
Morgan State University			Other	Other		
Morris College						B.A.
New York College Of Technology (CUNY)						A.A.
Norfolk State University						
North Carolina A&T State University						
North Carolina Central University	B.A.					
Oakwood College			B.A.			
Olive-Harvey College (CCC)						A.A., A.O.S.
Paine College			B.A.			
Paul Quinn College			B.A.			
Philander Smith College						
Prairie View A&M University						
Richard Daley College (CCC)						
Roxbury Community College						A.A.
Saint Augustine's College						
Saint Paul's College			B.A.			
Savannah State University	M.A.					
Selma University			B.A.			
Shaw University	B.A.		A.A., B.A., M.A.			
Shorter College						
Simmons Bible College			B.A.			
Sojourner Douglass College						
South Carolina State University						
Southern University and A&M College	Other					M.A.
Southern University at New Orleans	B.A.					
Southwestern Christian College			A.A., A.S., B.A., B.S.			
			B.A.			
Spelman College						
Talladega College	B.A.					
Tennesse State University	M.A., Ph.D.					
Texas College						
Texas Southern University						
Tougaloo College			A.A.			
Tuskegee University						
University of the District of Columbia	Other	A.S.			B.S.	B.S.
University of Maryland-Eastern Shore						B.S.
University of the Virgin Islands	Other					B.A.
Virginia State University						
Virginia Union University			B.A.			

Institution	Public Administration	Radiological Technology	Religion	Russian	Secretarial Science	Social Science
Virginia University of Lynchburg			B.A.			
West Virginia State University						
Wilberforce University						
Wiley College						
Winston-Salem State University						
Xavier University of Louisiana						
York College (CUNY)						

Majors and Degrees

Social Welfare/Social Work - Zoology

Institution	Social Welfare/Social Work	Sociology	Spanish	Technical Education	Theology	Urban Affairs	Veterinary Medicine	Zoology
Alabama A&M University		B.A.						
Alabama State University	B.S.	B.A.						
Albany State University	Other	B.A.	B.A.					
Alcorn State University		B.A.						
Allen University								
Arkansas Baptist College	B.S.W.							
Benedict College	B.S.	B.A.						
Bennett College								
Bethune-Cookman University		B.A.						
Bishop State Community College		B.A.						
Bluefield State College		B.A.						
Central State University	B.A.	B.A.						
Cheyney University of Pennsylvania		B.A.	Other					
Chicago State University	B.A.	B.A.						
Claflin University		B.A.						
Clark Atlanta University	B.S., M.S., Ph.D.	B.A., M.A.	B.A., M.A.					
Clinton Junior College								
Coahoma Community College								
Coppin State University	B.A.							
Dillard University		B.A.	B.A.			B.A.		
Edward Waters College		B.A.						
Elizabeth City State University	B.A.	B.A.						
Fayetteville State University	M.S.	B.A., M.A.						
Fisk University		B.A.	B.A.					
Florida A&M University	B.S.W., M.S.W.	B.A.	B.A.					
Florida Memorial University	B.S.W.	B.A.						
Fort Valley State University	Other	B.A.						
Gadsden State Community College		A.A.						
Grambling State University	B.A., M.S.	B.A.	B.A.					
Hampton University		B.S.						
Harold Washington College (CCC)								
Harry Truman College (CCC)								
Hinds Community College – Utica Campus								
Howard University	B.S.W., Ph.D.	B.A., Ph.D	B.A., M.A.					
Hutson-Tillotson University	B.A.	B.A.			B.A.			
Jarvis Christian College	B.S.	B.S.						
Johnson C. Smith University	B.S.W.	B.A.	B.A.					
Kennedy-King College (CCC)	A.A.	A.A.						
Kentucky State University	B.A.	Other						
Lane College		B.A.						
Langston University		B.A.						A.S.
Lawson State Community College		A.S.						
LeMoyne-Owen College	B.A.	B.A.						
Lincoln University (MO)		B.A., B.S., M.A.	B.A.					
Lincoln University (PA)		B.A., B.S.	B.A., B.S.					
Livingstone College	B.S.	B.A.						
Malcom X College (CCC)								
Martin University		B.A.						
Medgar Evers College (CUNY)								
Miles College	B.S.W.							
Mississippi Valley State University	B.S., M.S.	B.S.						
Morehouse College		B.A.						
Morehouse School of Medicine								
Morgan State University	B.A., M.A., Ph.D.	B.S., M.S.	Other			Other		
Morris College								
New York College Of Technology (CUNY)				A.A.				
Norfolk State University	B.A., M.A., Ph.D.	B.A.						
North Carolina A&T State University	B.S., M.S.	B.A.		B.S., M.S.				
North Carolina Central University	B.A.	B.A.						
Oakwood College	B.A.				B.A.			
Olive-Harvey College (CCC)								
Paine College		B.A.						
Paul Quinn College		B.A.						
Philander Smith College	B.A.	B.A.						
Prairie View A&M University	B.A.							
Richard Daley College (CCC)								
Roxbury Community College								
Saint Augustine's College								
Saint Paul's College	B.A.	B.A.						
Savannah State University	B.A., M.A.	B.A.				M.A.		
Selma University		A.A.						
Shaw University	B.A.	B.A.	B.A.					
Shorter College			A.A.					
Simmons Bible College					B.A.			
Sojourner Douglass College								
South Carolina State University		B.A.	B.A.					
Southern University and A&M College	B.S.	B.S.	B.A.					
Southern University at New Orleans	B.A., M.A.	B.A.						
Southwestern Christian College								
Spellman College		B.A.	B.A.					
Talladega College		B.A.						
Tennessee State University	B.A.	B.A.						
Texas College	B.A.							
Texas Southern University	B.A.	B.A. M.A.						
Tougaloo College		B.A.	B.A.					
Tuskegee University	B.A.	B.A.					B.S.	
University of the District of Columbia	B.A.	B.A.	B.A.			B.A.		
University of Maryland-Eastern Shore	B.S.	B.S.						
University of the Virgin Islands								
Virginia State University	B.A.	B.A.						
Virginia Union University	B.A.							

Institution	Social Welfare/Social Work	Sociology	Spanish	Technical Education	Theology	Urban Affairs	Veterinary Medicine	Zoology
Virginia University of Lynchburg		B.A.						
West Virginia State University	B.A.	B.A.						
Wilberforce University	B.A.	B.A.						
Wiley College								
Winston-Salem State University	B.S.	B.A.	B.A.					
Xavier University of Louisiana		B.A.	B.A.		B.A.			
York College (CUNY)		B.A.	B.A.					

Note: CCC denotes a City Colleges of Chicago institution
Sources: NAFEO Annual Membership Survey, 2007 and NAFEO member institutions

Additional Majors and Degrees

Table 5. Additional majors and degrees offered at NAFEO member institutions, Fall 2006

Institutions	Majors (and corresponding degrees)
Alabama State University	Computer Information Systems, B.S. Educational Leadership & Administration, M.Ed., Ed.D Health Information Management, B.S. Library Education Media, M.Ed. Marine Biology, B.S. Occupational Therapy, M.S.O.T. Parks & Recreation Management, B.S. Physical Education, B.S. School Counseling, M.Ed.
Albany State University	Business Information Systems, B.S. Educational Admin & Supervisor, E.DS., M.Ed. Forensic Science, B.S. Health & Physical Education, B.S., M.Ed. Mathematics, M.Ed. Middle Grades Education, M.Ed. Music, B.A., M.Ed. School Counseling, M.Ed. Science Education, B.S., M.Ed Technology Management, B.A.S.
Alcorn State University	Agribusiness Management, B.S. Agricultural Economics, B.S. Agricultural Science, B.S. Applied Science, B.S. Biotechnology, M.S. Child Development, B.S. Community College Instruction, M.A.T. Computer Network Information & Technology, B.S. Educational Psychology, B.S. General studies, B.A.
Allen University	Biology, B.S. Business Administration, B.A. Chemistry, B.S. English, B.S. Mathematics, B.S. Music, B.S. Social Sciences, B.S.
Benedict College	Child & Family Development, B.S. Computer Information Science, B.S. Environmental Health Science, B.S. Mass Communication, B.A. Public Health, B.S. Recreation, B.S.
Bethune-Cookman University	Computer Engineering, B.S. Hospitality Management, B.S. Speech Communication, B.A. Transformative Leadership, M.A.
Bluefield State College	Architectural Engineering Technology, A.A., B.S.ET Civil Engineering Technology, A.S., B.S.ET Electrical Engineering Technology, A.S., B.S.ET Mechanical Engineering Technology, A.S., B.S.ET Mining Engineering Technology, B.S.ET Regents, B.A.
Cheyney University of Pennsylvania	Music Merchandising, B.S.
Clark Atlanta University	African Women Studies, M.A., Ph.D. Community Counseling, M.A. Educational Leadership, M.A., Ed.D., Ed.S. Educational Studies, B.A. Fashion Design & Merchandising, B.A. Romance Languages, Ph.D. School Counseling, M.A. Speech Communication, B.A. Theater Arts, B.A.
Clinton Junior College	Liberal Arts, A.A.
Dillard University	International Business, B.A. Japanese Studies, B.A.
Elizabeth City State University	Aviation Sciences, B.S. Geology, B.S. Graphic Design, B.S. Industrial Technology, B.S. Marine Environmental Science, B.S. Pharmaceutical Sciences, B.S. Physical Education, B.S. School Administration, M.SA.

Institutions	Majors (and corresponding degrees)
Fayetteville State University	Biotechnology, *B.S.* Birth through Kindergarten, *B.S.* Educational Leadership, *Ed.D.* Fire Science, *B.S.* Forensic Science, *B.S.* Health Education, *B.S.* Middle Grades Education, *B.S.* Physical Education, *B.S.* School Administration, *M.SA.* Spanish, *B.A.*
Fort Valley State University	Agricultural Economics, *B.S.* Agricultural Engineering Technology, *B.S.* Commercial Design, *B.A.* Computer Information Systems, *B.A.* Environmental Health, *MPH* Guidance & Counseling, *M.S.* Liberal Studies, *B.A.* Mental Health Counseling, *M.S.* Rehabilitation Counseling, *M.S.* Veterinary Technology, *B.S.*
Grambling State University	Child Development, *A.S.* Computer Information Systems, *B.S.* Curriculum & Instruction, *Ed.D.* Educational Leadership, *Ed.D.* Hotel/Restaurant Management, *B.S.* Kinesiology, *B.S.* Leisure Studies, *B.S.* Liberal Arts, *M.A.* Paralegal Studies, *B.A.* Sports Administration, *M.S.*
Hampton University	Atmospheric Sciences, *M.S., Ph.D.* Nursing, *B.S., M.S., Ph.D.* Pharmacy, *PharmD.* Physical Therapy, *DPT.*
Harold Washington College (CCC)	Astronomy, *A.S.* Fine Arts, *A.S.* Geology, *A.S.* Humanities, *A.S.* Meteorology, *A.S.* Music, *A.S.* Photography, *A.A.S.* Physical Sciences, *A.S.* Social Sciences, *A.A.S.* Theatre, *A.A.S.*
Harris Stowe State University	Hospitality & Tourism Management, *B.S.* Information Sciences, *B.S.* Middle School/Junior High School Education, *B.S., Ed.D* Professional Interdisciplinary, *B.S.* Secondary Education, *B.S., Ed.D*
Harry Truman College (CCC)	Management / Marketing, *A.A.S.* Pre-Law, *A.A.*
Jarvis Christian College	Kinesiology, *B.S.*
Kentucky State University	Aquaculture/Aquatic Sciences, *M.A.* Child Development & Family Relations, *B.A.* Liberal Studies, *B.A., A.A.* Physical Education: *B.A.* Physical Education & Health (Teaching), *B.Sc.* Physical Education (Non-Teaching), *B.A.*
Langston University	Airway Science, *B.S.* Building Construction Management, *B.S.* Corrections, *B.S.* Crop & Soil Science, *B.S.* Entrepreneurship, *M.E.*, Health Administration, *B.S.* Health Physical Education, *B.S.* International Studies, *B.S.* Nutrition & Dietetics, *B.S.* Rehabilitation Counseling, *M.S.*
LeMoyne-Owen College	General Math Teacher Education, *B.S.* General Science Teacher Education, *B.S.* Humanities, *B.A.* Information Technology, *B.S.* Language Arts Teacher Education, *B.A.* Music, *B.A.* Social Studies Teacher Education, *B.A.*

Institutions	Majors (and corresponding degrees)
Lincoln University (MO)	Agribusiness, B.S. Applied Science in Technology, B.S. Civil Engineering Technology, B.S. Educational Leadership, Ed.S. Environmental Sciences, B.S. Guidance & Counseling, M.Ed. Liberal Studies, B.L.S. Physical Education, B.S. Sacred Music, B.S. Wellness, B.S.
Lincoln University (PA)	Actuarial Science, B.A., B.S. English Education, B.A., B.S. Environmental Sciences, B.A., B.S. General Sciences, B.A., B.S. Health & Physical Education, B.A., B.S. Industrial Psychology, B.A., B.S. International Relations, B.A., B.S. Japanese, B.S. Mathematics Education, B.A., B.S. Psycho-Biology, B.A., B.S.
Livingstone College	Law / History (Dual Degree), B.A. Law / Political Science (Dual Degree), B.A. Mathematics Education (K-12), B.S. Physical Education (K-12), B.S. Science / Engineering (Dual Degree), B.S. Sports Management, B.S. Theater Arts, B.A.
Malcolm X College (CCC)	Medicine, A.S. Natural & Behavioral Health, A.G.S. Pharmacology, A.S.
Mississippi Valley State University	Applied Technology & Technology Management, B.S. Bioinformatics, M.S. Communications, B.S. Environmental Health, B.S., M.S. Health, Physical Education & Recreation, B.S. Office Administration, B.S. Recording Industry, B.S. Rural Public Policy & Planning Speech, B.S. Teaching, M.A.T.
Morehouse School of Medicine	Biomedical Science, Ph.D. Clinical Research, M.S.C.R. Public Health, MPH Medicine, M.D.
North Carolina A&T State University	Computational Science, M.S.A. Energy & Environmental Studies, Ph.D. Geomatics, B.S. Leadership Studies, Ph.D. Liberal Studies, B.A. Occupational Safety, B.S. School Administration, M.S. Sports Science, B.S. Transportation, B.S.
Olive-Harvey College (CCC)	Marketing / Management, A.AA. Pharmacology, A.S. Physical Science, A.O.S. Pre-Law, A.A.
Richard Daley College (CCC)	Accounting, Certificate Program Business, Certificate Program Computer Science, Certificate Program Criminal Justice, Certificate Program Management, Certificate Program Marketing, Certificate Program Pharmacy, A.A. Speech, A.A.
Paine College	Broadcasting, B.A. Chemistry w/Environmental Science, B.S. Experimental Psychology, B.A. International Business, B.S. Management Information Systems, B.S. Middle Grades Education, B.S. Psychology w/Counseling, B.A. Public Relations, B.A. Social Psychology, B.A.
Savannah State University	Environmental Studies, B.S. Homeland Security, B.S. Information Systems, B.S. Marine Science, B.S., M.S. Performing Arts, B.A. Political Science, B.S. Recreation & Park Administration, B.S.

Institutions	Majors (and corresponding degrees)
Southern University and A&M College	Agriculture Economics, B.S.
	Agriculture Sciences, B.S.
	E-Business, B.A.
	Family & Consumer Sciences, B.S.
	Fine Arts, B.A.
	Mass Communications, B.A., M.A.
	Middle School Education, B.S.
	Speech Communications, B.A.
	Theatre Arts, B.A.
	Urban Forestry, B.S., M.S., Ph.D.
Southern University at New Orleans	Business Entrepreneurship, B.S.
	Child Development & Family Studies, B.A.
	General Studies, BGS.
	Museum Studies and Cultural Preservation, M.A.
	Substance Abuse, A.A., B.A.
University of the District of Columbia	Administration of Justice, B.A.
	Biology, B.A.
	Child Development & Nursery, A.A.
	Corrections Administration, AAS
	Graphic Communications Technology, A.AS.
	Graphic Design, A.A.
	Health Education, B.S.
	Nutrition & Food Science, B.S.
	Urban Studies, B.A.
	Water Quality & Marine Science, A.AS.
University of Maryland-Eastern Shore	Applied Design, B.A.
	Aviation Science, B.S.
	Environmental Science, B.S.
	Exercise Science, B.S.
	Guidance & Counseling, M.S.
	Hotel & Restaurant Management, B.S.
	Marine Estuarine Environmental Science, M.S., Ph.D.
	Physicians Assistant, B.S.
	Rehabilitation Services, B.S., M.S.
	Technology, B.S., M.S.
University of the Virgin Islands	Computer Information Systems, A.A.
	Environmental Science, M.S.
	Hotel & Restaurant Management, A.A.
	Marine Biology, B.A, B.S., M.S.
	Police Science & Administration, A.A.
	Processed Technology, A.AS.
	Speech Communication, B.A.
	Theater, B.A.
Winston-Salem State University	Art Education, B.A.
	Biotechnology, B.S.
	Clinical Laboratory Science, B.S.
	Computer Programming, Certificate P.B.
	Exercise Science, B.S.
	Information Technology, B.S.
	Interdisciplinary Studies, B.S.
	Mass Communications, B.A.
	Rehabilitation Counseling, B.S., M.S.
	Teaching English as a 2nd Language, M.A.

Note: CCC denotes a City Colleges of Chicago institution
Sources: NAFEO Annual Membership Survey, 2007 and NAFEO member institutions

Special Programs at HBCUs and PBIs

Table 6. Centers of Excellence at NAFEO member institutions, Fall 2006

Institution	Centers of Excellence
Alabama State University	Center for Research Excellence in Science and Technology
Albany State University	Center for Excellence in Teaching/Learning/Advising Early Learning Center Center for Entrepreneurship Telecommunications Center
Alcorn State University	Center for Swine Research Production and Marketing Center for Rural Life and Economic Development
Benedict College	Equity and Education of African Americans
Clark Atlanta University	School of Business Computation & National Security Urban Education Communications Arts
Grambling State University	Center for Mathematical Achievement in Science and Technology (CMAST)
Hampton University	Center for Teaching Excellence (CTE)
Langston University	E. (Kika) de la Garza Center for Goat Research Center for Biotechnical Research and Education Grasslands Center for Excellence
Morgan State University	Center For Excellence in Mathematics and Science
North Carolina A&T State University	Battlefield Capability Enhancement
Savannah State University	Marine Science Computer Information Systems
University of Maryland Eastern Shore	Hotel & Restaurant Management Professional Golf Management Aviation Science Food Science & Technology Center
Winston-Salem State University	Center of Health Services Center of Science and Technology Center of Financial Services Center of Teaching and Learning

Source: NAFEO Annual Membership Survey, 2007

Table 7. Goods produced and services offered at NAFEO member institutions, Fall 2006

Institution	Goods produced and services offered
Alcorn State University	Wine Pepper Sauce Cookies Potatoes Vegetables Muscadine grapes Hot peppers Soy Yams Greens Peas Corn
Fort Valley State University	Meat Products Dairy Products Seafood Goat Meat Goat Cheese Freshwater Shrimp
Langston University	Goat Milk Goat Cheese Goat Ice cream
University of Maryland-Eastern Shore	Broilers Pigs Goats Sheep Corn Wheat Hay Soybeans GIS Services Posters
University of the Virgin Islands	Senepol cattle Sheep (crossbred lamb) Fish Fruits Vegetables

Source: NAFEO Annual Membership Survey, 2007

Table 8. NAFEO member institutions with patents pending, Fall 2006

Institution	Patents pending
North Carolina A&T State University	Fire Resistant Core Materials High-Sensitivity Differential Pressure Transducer Recombinant Protein V Fiber-Optic Biosensor

Source: NAFEO Annual Membership Survey, 2007

Table 9. NAFEO member institutions with programs or services exclusively provided to service the surrounding community, Fall 2006

Institution	Program or service
Alabama State University	Science in Motion Small Business Development Center Technology in Motion Alabama Reading Initiative Program Zelia Stephens Early Childhood Center
Albany State University	NASA Science, Engineering, Mathematics, and Aerospace Academy Project
Alcorn State University	Traceway Community Development Corporation
Benedict College	Child Development Center Business & Economic Development Center Benedict College Community Involvement Initiative
Bethune-Cookman University	Transformative Leadership Program Web-based GIS-Enabled Programs
Dillard University	Environmental Health Science Worker Training Program
Elizabeth City State University	Community Development
Fort Valley State University	The Cooperative Extension Program
Harris-Stowe State University	Upward Bound Educational Talent Search
LeMoyne-Owen College	HBCU Wellness Project
Livingstone College	HUD First Time Home Buyer/Owner Program
Mississippi Valley State University	Delta Research and Cultural Institute
Rust College	Families First
Southern University and A&M College	Minority Workers Program Full-Time Fathers Program Empowering Youth Choices Building Stronger Families Timbuktu Academy
Southern University at New Orleans	Program for Excellence in Science, Mathematics, and Computer Technology (PESMaCT) College of Education Charter School Program
Southwestern Christian College	Upward Bound
Talladega College	Upward Bound
Winston-Salem State University	Center for Community Safety Community Knowledge Centers Small Business and Technology Development Center S.G. Atkins Community Development Center

Source: NAFEO Annual Membership Survey, 2007

Table 10. Special Research Centers at NAFEO member institutions, Fall 2006

Institution	Special Research Center
Alabama State University	The Center of Leadership and Public Policy
Alcorn State University	Mississippi River Research Center Center for Rural Life and Economic Development Bio-Technology Center
Cheyney University of Pennsylvania	Aqua/Fisheries Farm
Elizabeth City State University	Computational Science—Scientific Visualization (CSSV) lab Center of Excellence in Remote Sensing Education and Research (CERSER)
Fort Valley State University	Population Studies Center Aquaculture Program Georgia Goat Research and Extension Center
Hampton University	Center for Atmospheric Sciences Center for Advanced Medical Institution Center for Laser Science & Spectroscopy Center for the Study of the Origin and Structure of Matter (COSM) Hampton - Penn Nursing Center
Kentucky State University	Center of Excellence for Study of Kentucky African Americans Kentucky Program of Distinction
Langston University	E. (Kika) de la Garza Institute for Goat Research
LeMoyne-Owen College	Minority Scientific Research
Lincoln University of Missouri	Foster Hall
Mississippi Valley State University	Delta Research and Cultural Institute Sponsored Research for the Sciences
Morgan State University	Biomedical Research Center for Health Disparities Drug Abuse Research Estuarine Research Center Institute of Urban Research
North Carolina A&T State University	Public Health Advanced Materials & Nanotechnology Computational Science & Engineering Leadership & Community Development
Savannah State University	Center for Graduate Studies and Sponsored Research
Southern University and A&M College	Center for Social Research Capital Small Business Development Center Center for Energy and Environmental Studies Health Research Center Urban Recreation Research Center
Talladega College	Historically Black Colleges and Universities Undergraduate Program (HBCU-UP)
University of the District of Columbia	Center for Applied Research and Urban Policy
University of Maryland Eastern Shore	Soybean Research Center Farm and Animal Center Agribusiness Research Center Hydroponics Greenhouse Swine Research Center
University of the Virgin Islands	Virgin Islands Experimental Program to Stimulate Competitive Research (VI-EPSCoR) CMES Center for Marine and Environment Agricultural Experimental Station Eastern Caribbean Center
Winston-Salem State University	Biomedical Research Infrastructure Center

Source: NAFEO Annual Membership Survey, 2007

Table 11. Special Research Libraries at NAFEO member institutions, Fall 2006

Institution	Special Research Library
Alcorn State University	School of Nursing
Langston University	Melvin B. Tolson Black Heritage Center
North Carolina A&T State University	Contained within areas of Research Cluster
Paine College	Paine College Archives and Major Field Papers
Southern University and A&M College	John B. Cade Library Architecture Library Law School Library
Southern University at New Orleans	SUNO Archive

Table 12. Special Collections at NAFEO member institutions, Fall 2006

Institution	Special Collection
Alabama State University	Ollie L. Brown Afro - American Heritage Collection E. D. Nixon Collection Collection of the Montgomery Improvement Association Levi Watkins Collections
Albany State University	Black Collectives
Bethune-Cookman University	Mary McLeod Bethune Rosewood Florida
Cheyney University of Pennsylvania	Ethnic Collection Archives Collection
Dillard University	Patton Collection
Elizabeth City State University	Hugh Cale Collection Evelyn A. Johnson Collection Murrill Collection Photo Collection
Fort Valley State University	Alfonso Biggs Collection
Hampton University	Peabody Collection Governmental Papers
Harris-Stowe State University	William Clay Papers Wolfe Jazz Collection
Jarvis Christian College	Texas Christian Mission Fellowship Papers
Kentucky State University	Kentucky African Americans collection
LeMoyne-Owen College	Sweeney Collection
Lincoln University	Books and Journals
Livingstone College	Heritage Hall Artifacts
North Carolina A&T State University	The Mattye Reid African Heritage Collection The Henry Clinton Taylor Collection
Rust College	Ronald Trojcak Collection The Inuit Collection
Southern University and A&M College	Camile Shade African American Collection Music Listening Archives
Southern University at New Orleans	Dr. Robert Gex Collection Dr. William & Jane Bertrand Collection Dr. & Mrs. Pascal Imperato Collection John & Gail Povey Collection
Talladega College	Amistad Murals Bunker Collection Henry Drewry Collection African Missionary Collection
University of Maryland Eastern Shore	Hytche History & Legacy Somerset County Collections Maryland Collections
University of the Virgin Islands	Ralf de Chabert Collection Melchior Center

Source: NAFEO Annual Membership Survey, 2007

Table 13. Online Degree Programs offered at NAFEO member institutions, Fall 2006

Institution	Online Degree Program
Albany State University	Nursing, *M.S.*
	Technology Management, *B.AS.*
Alcorn State University	Workforce Education Leadership, *M.S.*
Bethune-Cookman University	Transformative Leadership, *M.A.*
Bluefield State University	Radiologic Sciences, *B.S.*
Hampton University	Continuing Studies, *B.S.*
	Nursing, *M.S., Ph.D.*
	Religious Studies, *B.S.*
Kentucky State University	Special Education, *B.A.*
Lincoln University (MO)	Nursing, *B.S.*
North Carolina A&T State University	Adult Education, *M.S.*
	Agriculture Education, *B.S., M.S.*
	Business Education, *B.S.*
	Health & Physical Education, *M.S.*
	Instructional Technology, *M.S.*
Southern University and A&M College	Rehabilitation Services, *M.S.*
Southern University at New Orleans	Criminal Justice, *B.S.*
	Early Childhood Education, *B.S.*
	General Studies, *B.G.S.*
	Museum Studies, *M.A.*
Southwestern Christian College	Bible, *B.S.*
Winston-Salem State University	Clinical Laboratory, *B.S.*
	Integrative Studies, *B.A.*
	Physical Education, *Lateral*
	Rehabilitation Counseling, *M.S.*

Source: NAFEO Annual Membership Survey, 2007

Table 14. Continuing Education Programs at NAFEO member institutions, Fall 2006

Institution	Continuing Education Program
Alabama State University	Professional Development Workshops Finance, Career, and Test Preparation Money Management Personal Finance Technology/Computer Skills Self-Enrichment: Home, Leisure and Fitness
Albany State University	Summer Outreach Program for youth ages 5 to 18 Kiddy College Young Scholars Academy of Excellence Workforce Development courses Pre-planning and planning conferences/workshops/seminars.
Alcorn State University	Courses and programs on the Mississippi Electronic Campus (e-Campus)
Allen University	School for Professional Adults (SPA)
Bethune-Cookman University	Professional Studies
Fort Valley State University	Horseback riding lessons Home buyer/landlord lessons Conversational Spanish classes
Jarvis Christian College	Education
Kentucky State University	The University offers career and professional development opportunities to people within Central Kentucky service area through a wide range of on-campus, distance-learning environments including ITV and TV
LeMoyne-Owen College	Teacher Education Licensure Certification
Lincoln University of Missouri	Courses offered by State of Missouri Departments of Conservation and Natural Resources
Livingstone College	Baccalaureate Degree Programs in Criminal Justice, Business Administration, Elementary Education and Religious Studies
Mississippi Valley State University	Evening and weekend college
North Carolina A&T State University	Evening College
Rust College	Adult Pathway
Southern University and A&M College	Add-on certification in Special Education
University of the District of Columbia	General Office Skills Computer Technology Training Professional & Business Development Occupational Skills Customer Service
Winston-Salem State University	Paralegal Advocacy Certificate Course Legal Investigation Certificate Course Legal Secretary Certificate Course

Source: NAFEO Annual Membership Survey, 2007

Table 15. Distance Learning Courses offered at NAFEO member institutions, Fall 2006

Institution	Distance Learning Course
Alabama State University	Educational Research Computer-Based Instructional Technology Current and Emerging Instructional Technology Integration of Technology K-12
Alcorn State University	Graduate Nursing Courses Graduate Business Courses
Cheyney University of Pennsylvania	Professional Human Growth & Development Behavior Modification in Education
Elizabeth City State University	Management Information System Quantitative methods (Business Administration) Managerial Accounting General Psychology Teaching reading in content area (Education) Instructional Technology Multicultural Education Foundations of Education Secondary Instructional Methods (Education) Introduction to Computer Instructional Technology (Education)
Grambling State University	Methods of Justice Research Prison Subcultures Nature & Needs of Development Learners Education Management & Evaluation Civil Litigation II Advanced Program Evaluation Online Writing & Design Introduction to Mass Communication History & Philosophy of Higher Education Problems and Issues in Development Seminar
Harris-Stowe State University	Urban Development Introduction to Logical Thinking Introduction to Ethics Introduction to Philosophy Introduction to Science Survey Physical Science Survey Professional Development of Managers Management Information Systems Digital Networks End User Database
Jarvis Christian College	Speech Biology History
Kentucky State University	Fish Genetics Accounting Information Systems Principles of Accounting I Principles of Aquaculture Introduction to Art Computer Information Systems Methods and Strategies in Behavior Management The Ancient World
Mississippi Valley State University	Compressed Video
Paine College	Philosophy 230 English 101 English 102 English 232 English 333 Business Administration 231 Farsi 220 Pashto 220 Philosophy 240 Religion 230
Southern University and A&M College	Stuttering: Diagnosis & Management Medical and Psychological Aspects of Disabilities Introduction to Rehabilitation Counseling Measurement and Evaluation of Atypical Children Characteristics of Children with M/M Learning Disorder Behavioral Approaches to Managing Children with LD Methods in Teaching Academic Subjects to M/M children Teaching Vocational skills to M/M learners Freshmen Composition Fundamentals of Family Financial Planning

Institution	Distance Learning Course
Southern University at New Orleans	Introduction to Biology I & II Introductory Chemistry Introduction to Early Childhood College Mathematics College Algebra Introduction to Philosophy Introduction to Logic The U.S. to 1865 The U.S. since 1865 American Government
Southwestern Christian College	Old Testament Survey 121 New Testament Survey 122 New Testament Church 331 Restoration Movement 436 Life and Teachings of Christ 221 Prison and Pastoral Epistles 222 Christian Ethics 330 Revelation 430 General Psychology 131 Sociology 133
Talladega College	Communications Mathematics Computer Science
University of Maryland Eastern Shore	Information Literacy Intro to Criminal Justice Intro to Sociology Basic Composition II Social Problems Fundamentals of Family Financial Plan Technical Writing Development Psychology Hotel Management and Operations Introduction to Development Disabilities
University of the Virgin Islands	Computer Information System Computer Science English Nursing Paralegal Science Theater Communication Criminal Justice

Source: NAFEO Annual Membership Survey, 2007

Table 16. NAFEO member institutions with ROTC affiliations, Fall 2006

Institution	ROTC Affiliation
Alabama State University	Air Force
Albany State University	Army
Alcorn State University	Army
Allen University	Army
Benedict College	Army
Bethune-Cookman University	Army
Cheyney University of Pennsylvania	Army (in conjunction with West Chester University)
Clark Atlanta University	Army, Air Force (in conjunction with cooperating institutions)
Dillard University	Army, Air Force
Elizabeth City State University	Army
Fort Valley State University	Army
Grambling State University	Army
Hampton University	Army, Navy
Harris-Stowe State University	Army
Kentucky State University	Air Force, Army
Langston University	Air Force, Army
Lincoln University (MO)	Army
Lincoln University (PA)	Army
Livingstone College	Army (in conjunction with the University of North Carolina-Charlotte)
Mississippi Valley State University	Army
North Carolina A&T State University	Air Force, Army
Paine College	Army
Savannah State University	Army, Navy
Southern University and A&M College	Army, Navy, Air Force (in conjunction with Louisiana State University)
University of the District of Columbia	Air Force, Army
University of the Virgin Islands	Army
Winston-Salem State University	Army

Source: NAFEO Annual Membership Survey, 2007

Table 17. **NAFEO Member Land-Grant Institutions**

Institution	Year established
Alabama A&M University	1875
Alcorn State University	1871
Delaware State University	1891
Florida A&M University	1887
Fort Valley State University	1895
Kentucky State University	1886
Langston University	1897
Lincoln University (MO)	1890
North Carolina A&T State University	1891
Prairie View A&M University	1876
South Carolina State University	1896
Southern University and A&M College	1880
Tennessee State University	1912
Tuskegee University	1881
University of Arkansas – Pine Bluff	1873
University of the District of Columbia	1977
University of Maryland – Eastern Shore	1886
University of the Virgin Islands	1962
Virginia State University	1882
West Virginia State University	1891

Law Schools at NAFEO Member Institutions, 2008

Florida A&M University
Leroy Pernell, Dean
College of Law
201 Beggs Avenue
Orlando, Florida 32801
www.famu.edu/law

Howard University
Kurt L. Schmoke, Dean
School of Law
2900 Van Ness Street NW
Washington, DC 20008
www.law.howard.edu

North Carolina Central University
Raymond C. Pierce, Dean
School of Law
640 Nelson Street
Durham, North Carolina 27707
web.nccu.edu/law

Southern University and A&M College
Judge Freddie Pitcher, Jr., Chancellor
Southern University Law Center
P.O. Box 9294
Baton Rouge, Louisiana 70813
www.sulc.edu

Texas Southern University
McKen Carrington, Dean
Thurgood Marshall School of Law
3100 Cleburne Street
Houston, Texas 77004
www.tsu.edu/academics/law

University of the District of Columbia
Katherine S. Broderick, Dean
David A. Clarke School of Law
4200 Connecticut Avenue NW
Washington, DC 20008
www.law.udc.edu

NAFEO Member Institution Directory, by state

Alabama

Alabama A&M University
Dr. Robert Jennings, President
P.O. Box 1357
Normal, Alabama 35762
www.aamu.edu
Public

Alabama State University
Dr. Joe A. Lee, President
P.O. Box 271
Montgomery, Alabama 36101
www.alasu.edu
Public

Bishop State Community College
Dr. Yvonne Kennedy, President
351 North Broad Street
Mobile, Alabama 36603
www.bscc.cc.al.us
Public

Concordia College
Dr. Julius Jenkins, President
1804 Green Street
Selma, Alabama 36701
www.concordiaselma.edu
Private

Gadsden State Community College
Dr. Renee Culverhouse, President
P.O. Box 227
Gadsden, Alabama 35902
www.gadsdenstate.edu
Public

H. Councill Trenholm State Technical College
Dr. Sam Munnerlyn, President
1225 Air Base Boulevard
Montgomery, Alabama 36108
www.trenholmtech.cc.al.us
Public

J.F. Drake State Technical College
Dr. Helen T. McAlpine, President
3421 Meridian Street North
Huntsville, Alabama 35811
http://www.dstc.cc.al.us/index.html
Public

Lawson State Community College
Dr. Perry W. Ward, President
3060 Wilson Road S.W.
Birmingham, Alabama 35221
www.ls.cc.al.us
Public

Miles College
Dr. George French, Jr., President
5500 Myron Massey Boulevard
Fairfield, Alabama 35064
www.miles.edu
Private

Oakwood College
Dr. Delbert Baker, President
7000 Adventist Boulevard
Huntsville, Alabama 35896
www.oakwood.edu
Private

Shelton State Community College
Dr. Rick Rogers, President
9500 Old Greensboro Road
Tuscaloosa, Alabama 35405
www.sheltonstate.edu
Public

Stillman College
Dr. Ernest McNealey, President
P.O. Box 1430
Tuscaloosa, Alabama 35403
www.stillman.edu
Private

Talladega College
Dr. Oscar L. Prater, President
627 West Battle Street
Talladega, Alabama 35160
www.talladega.edu
Private

Tuskegee University
Dr. Benjamin F. Payton, President
Tuskegee, Alabama 36088
www.tuskegee.edu
Private

Arkansas

Arkansas Baptist College
Dr. Fitz Hill, President
1621 Martin Luther King Drive
Little Rock, Arkansas 72202
www.arkansasbaptist.edu
Private

Philander Smith College
Dr. Walter M. Kimbrough, President
One Trudie Kibbe Reed Drive
Little Rock, Arkansas 72202
www.philander.edu
Private

Shorter College
Dr. Cora D. McHenry, President
604 Locust Street
North Little Rock, Arkansas 72114
www.shorter.edu
Private

University of Arkansas at Pine Bluff
Dr. Lawrence A. Davis, Jr., Chancellor
1200 North University
Pine Bluff, Arkansas 71601
www.uapb.edu
Public

California

Charles R. Drew University
Dr. Susan Kelly, President
1731 East 120th Street
Los Angeles, California 90059
www.cdrewu.edu
Private

District of Columbia

Howard University
Dr. H. Patrick Swygert, President
2400 Sixth Street NW
Washington, DC 20059
www.howard.edu
Private

University of the District of Columbia
Dr. William L. Pollard, President
4200 Connecticut Avenue NW
Washington, DC 20008
www.udc.edu
Public

Delaware

Delaware State University
Dr. Allen L. Sessoms, President
1200 North DuPont Highway
Dover, Delaware 19901
www.desu.edu
Public

Florida

Bethune-Cookman University
Dr. Trudie Kibbe Reed, President
640 Dr. Mary McLeod Bethune Boulevard
Daytona Beach, Florida 32114
www.bethune.cookman.edu
Private

Edward Waters College
Dr. Claudette Williams, President
1658 Kings Road
Jacksonville, Florida 32209
www.ewc.edu
Private

Florida Agricultural and Mechanical University
Dr. James H. Ammons, President
400 Lee Hall
Tallahassee, Florida 32307
www.famu.edu
Public

Florida Memorial University
Dr. Karl Wright, President
15800 NW 42nd Avenue
Miami, Florida 33054
www.fmc.edu

Georgia

Albany State University
Dr. Everette Freeman, President
504 College Drive
Albany, Georgia 31705
www.asurams.edu
Public

Clark Atlanta University
Dr. Walter D. Broadnax, President
223 James P. Brawley Drive SW
Atlanta, Georgia 30314
www.cau.edu
Private

Fort Valley State University
Dr. Larry E. Rivers, President
1005 State University Drive
Fort Valley, Georgia 31030
www.fvsu.edu
Public

Interdenominational Theological Center
Dr. Michael A. Battle, President
700 Martin Luther King Drive SW
Atlanta, Georgia 30314
www.itc.edu
Private

Morehouse College
Dr. Robert Michael Franklin, Jr., President
830 Westview Drive SW
Atlanta, Georgia 30314
www.morehouse.edu
Private

Morehouse School of Medicine
Dr. John E. Maupin, DDS/MBA, President
720 Westview Drive SW
Atlanta, Georgia 30310
www.msm.edu
Private

Morris Brown College
Dr. Pritchett Stanley, President
643 Martin Luther King Drive NW
Atlanta, Georgia 30314
www.morrisbrown.edu
Private

Paine College
Dr. George C. Bradley, President
1235 15th Street
Augusta, Georgia 30901
www.paine.edu
Private

Savannah State University
Dr. Earl G. Yarbrough, Sr., President
P.O. Box 20449
Savannah, Georgia 31404
www.savstate.edu
Public

Spelman College
Dr. Beverly Daniel Tatum, President
350 Spelman Lane SW, Box 616
Atlanta, Georgia 30314
www.spelman.edu
Private

Illinois

Chicago State University
Dr. Elnora Daniel, President
9501 South King Drive
Chicago, Illinois 60628
www.csu.edu
Public

City Colleges of Chicago
Dr. Wayne Watson, Chancellor
226 West Jackson, 14th Floor
Chicago, Illinois 60606
www.ccc.edu
Public

Kennedy-King College
Mr. Clyde El-Amin, President
6800 South Wentworth Avenue
Chicago, Illinois 60621
http://kennedyking.cc.edu
Public

Indiana

Martin University
Dr. Algeania Freeman, President
2171 Avondale Place
Indianapolis, Indiana 46218
www.martin.edu
Private

Kentucky

Kentucky State University
Dr. Mary Evans Sias, President
400 East Main Street
Frankfort, Kentucky 40601
www.kysu.edu
Public

Simmons Bible College
Dr. Kevin Cosby, President
1811 Dumesnil Street
Louisville, Kentucky 40210
www.simmonscollegeky.edu
Private

Louisiana

Dillard University
Dr. Marvalene Hughes, President
New Orleans, Louisiana 70122
www.dillard.edu
Private

Grambling State University
Dr. Horace A. Judson, President
403 Main Street
Grambling, Louisiana 71245
www.gram.edu
Public

Southern University and A&M College
Dr. Edward R. Jackson, Chancellor
P.O. Box 9374, SU Branch Post Office
Baton Rouge, Louisiana 70813
www.subr.edu
Public

Southern University at New Orleans
Dr. Victor Ukpolo, Chancellor
6400 Press Drive
New Orleans, Louisiana 70126
www.suno.edu
Public

Southern University System
Dr. Ralph Slaughter, President
Baton Rouge, Louisiana 70813
www.sus.edu
Public

Southern University, Shreveport Bossier Campus
Dr. Ray L. Belton, Chancellor
3050 Martin Luther King, Jr. Drive
Shreveport, Louisiana 71107
www.susla.edu
Public

Xavier University of Louisiana
Dr. Norman Francis, President
1 Drexel Drive
New Orleans, Louisiana 70125
www.xula.edu
Private

Massachusetts

Roxbury Community College
Dr. Terrence Gomes, President
1234 Columbus Avenue
Roxbury Crossing, Massachusetts 02120
www.rcc.mass.edu
Public

Maryland

Bowie State University
Dr. Mickey Burnim, President
14000 Jericho Park Road
Bowie, Maryland 20715
www.bowiestate.edu
Public

Coppin State University
Dr. Sadie Gregory, Interim President
2500 West North Avenue
Baltimore, Maryland 21216
www.coppin.edu
Public

Morgan State University
Dr. Earl S. Richardson, President
1700 Cold Spring Lane
Baltimore, Maryland 21251
www.morgan.edu
Public

Sojourner Douglass College
Dr. Charles W. Simmons, President
500 Caroline Street
Baltimore, Maryland 21205
www.sdc.edu
Private

University of Maryland—Eastern Shore
Dr. Thelma Thompson, President
Princess Anne, Maryland 21853
www.umes.edu
Public

Michigan

Lewis College of Business
Dr. Walter McMurty, President
17370 Meyers Road
Detroit, Michigan 48235
www.lewiscollege.edu
Private

Missouri

Harris-Stowe State University
Dr. Henry Givens, Jr., President
3026 Laclede Avenue
Saint Louis, Missouri 63103
http://www.hssu.edu/
Public

Lincoln University of Missouri
Dr. Carolyn Mahoney, President
820 Chestnut Street
Jefferson City, Missouri 65102
www.lincolnu.edu
Public

Mississippi

Alcorn State University
Dr. Malvin A. Williams, Interim President
1000 ASU Drive #359
Lorman, Mississippi 39096
www.alcorn.edu
Public

Coahoma Community College
Dr. Vivian M. Presley, President
3240 Friars Point Road
Clarksdale, Mississippi 38614
www.coahomacc.edu
Public

Hinds Community College—Utica Campus
Dr. George E. Barnes, Vice President
P.O. Box 1003 Hwy 18
Utica, Mississippi 39175
www.hindscc.edu
Public

Jackson State University
Dr. Ronald Mason, Jr., President
1400 J.R. Lynch Street
Jackson, Mississippi 39217
www.jsums.edu
Public

Mississippi Valley State University
Dr. Lester C. Newman, President
14000 Highway 82 West, Box 7272
Itta Bena, Mississippi 38941
www.mvsu.edu
Public

Rust College
Dr. David Beckley, President
150 Rust Avenue
Holly Springs, Mississippi 38635
www.rustcollege.edu
Private

Tougaloo College
Dr. Beverly W. Hogan, President
500 West County Line Road
Tougaloo, Mississippi 39174
www.tougaloo.edu
Private

North Carolina

Barber Scotia College
Dr. Carl Flamer, President
145 Cabarrus Avenue
Concord, North Carolina 28025
www.b-sc.edu
Private

Bennett College
Dr. Julianne Malveaux, President
900 East Washington Street
Greensboro, North Carolina 27401
www.bennett.edu
Private

Elizabeth City State University
Dr. Willie Gilchrist, Chancellor
1704 Weeksville Road
Eilzabeth City, North Carolina 27909
www.ecsu.edu
Public

Fayetteville State University
Dr. Lloyd V. "Vic" Hackley, Interim Chancellor
1200 Murchison Road
Fayetteville, North Carolina 28301
www.uncfsu.edu
Public

Johnson C. Smith University
Dr. Dorothy C. Yancy, President
100 Beatties Ford Road
Charlotte, North Carolina 28216
www.jcsu.edu
Private

Livingstone College
Dr. Jimmy R. Jenkins, Sr., President
701 West Monroe Street
Salisbury, North Carolina 28144
www.livingstone.edu
Private

North Carolina Agricultural and Technical State University
Dr. Stanley F. Battle, Chancellor
1601 East Market Street
Greensboro, North Carolina 27411
www.ncat.edu
Public

North Carolina Central University
Dr. Charlie Nelms, Chancellor
1801 Fayetteville Street
Durham, North Carolina 27707
www.nccu.edu
Public

Saint Augustine's College
Dr. Dianne Boardley Suber, President
1315 Oakwood Avenue
Raleigh, North Carolina 27610
www.st-aug.edu
Private

Shaw University
Dr. Clarence G. Newsome, President
118 East South Street
Raleigh, North Carolina 27601
www.shawuniversity.edu
Private

Winston-Salem State University
Dr. Donald Reaves, Chancellor
200 Blair Hall
Winston-Salem, North Carolina 27110
www.wssu.edu
Public

New York

Medgar Evers College
Dr. Edison O. Jackson, President
1650 Bedford Avenue
Brooklyn, New York 11225
www.mec.cuny.edu
Public

New York City College of Technology
Dr. Russell K. Hotzler, President
300 Jay Street
Brooklyn, New York 11201
www.citytech.cuny.edu
Public

York College/The City University of New York
Dr. Marcia V. Keizs, President
94-20 Guy R. Brewer Boulevard
Jamaica, New York 11451
www.york.cuny.edu
Public

Ohio

Central State University
Mr. John Garland, President
1400 Brush Row Road
Wilberforce, Ohio 45384
www.centralstate.edu
Public

Cuyahoga Community College
Dr. Jerry Sue Thornton, President
700 Carnegie Avenue
Cleveland, Ohio 44115
www.tri-c.edu
Public

Wilberforce University
Dr. Floyd H. Flake, President
1055 North Bickett Road
Wilberforce, Ohio 45384
www.wilberforce.edu
Private

Oklahoma

Langston University
Dr. JoAnn Haysbert, President
P.O. Box 907
Langston, Oklahoma 73050
www.lunet.edu
Public

Pennsylvania

Cheyney University of Pennsylvania
Dr. Michelle Howard-Vital, President
1837 University Circle
Cheyney, Pennsylvania 19319
www.cheyney.edu
Public

Lincoln University
Dr. Ivory V. Nelson, President
P.O. Box 179
Lincoln University, Pennsylvania 19352
www.lincoln.edu
Public

South Carolina

Allen University
Dr. Charles E. Young, President
1530 Harden Street
Columbia, South Carolina 29204
www.allenuniversity.edu
Private

Benedict College
Dr. David H. Swinton, President
1600 Harden Street
Columbia, South Carolina 29204
www.benedict.edu
Private

Claflin University
Dr. Henry N. Tisdale, President
400 Magnolia Street
Orangeburg, South Carolina 29115
www.claflin.edu
Private

Clinton Junior College
Dr. Elaine Johnson-Copeland, President
1029 Crawford Road
Rock Hill, South Carolina 29730
www.clintonjuniorcollege.edu
Private

Denmark Technical College
Dr. John K. Waddell, President
P.O. Box 327
Denmark, South Carolina 29042
www.denmarktech.edu
Public

Morris College
Dr. Luns Richardson, President
100 West College Street
Sumter, South Carolina 29150
www.morris.edu
Private

South Carolina State University
Dr. Leonard McIntyre, Interim President
300 College Street NE
Orangeburg, South Carolina 29117
www.scsu.edu
Public

Voorhees College
Dr. Lee Monroe, Jr., President
481 Porter Road
Denmark, South Carolina 29042
www.voorhees.edu
Private

Tennessee

Fisk University
Dr. Hazel O'Leary, President
1000 17th Avenue North
Nashville, Tennessee 37208
www.fisk.edu
Private

Lane College
Dr. Wesley McClure, President
545 Lane Avenue
Jackson, Tennessee 38301
www.lanescollege.edu
Public

Le Moyne-Owen College
Dr. Johnnie B. Watson, Interim President
807 Walker Avenue
Memphis, Tennessee 38126
http://www.loc.edu/
Private

Meharry Medical College
Dr. Wayne J. Riley, President
1005 D.B. Todd Boulevard
Nashville, Tennessee 37208
www.mmc.edu
Private

Tennessee State University
Dr. Melvin N. Johnson, D.B.A., President
3500 John. A. Merrit Boulevard
Nashville, Tennessee 37209
www.tnstate.edu
Public

Texas

Huston-Tillotson University
Dr. Larry L. Earvin, President
900 Chicon Street
Austin, Texas 78702
www.htu.edu
Private

Jarvis Christian College
Dr. Sebetha Jenkins, President
P.O. Box 1470
Hawkins, Texas 75765
www.jarvis.edu
Private

Paul Quinn College
Michael J. Sorrell, J.D., President
3837 Simpson Stuart Road
Dallas, Texas 75241
www.pqc.edu
Private

Prairie View A&M University
Dr. George C. Wright, President
P.O. Box 519
Prairie View, Texas 77446
www.pvamu.edu
Public

Southwestern Christian College
Dr. Jack Evans, Sr., President
P.O. Box 10
Terrell, Texas 75160
www.swcc.edu
Private

Texas College
Dr. Billy C. Hawkins, President
2404 North Grand Avenue
Tyler, Texas 75702
www.texascollege.edu
Private

Texas Southern University
Dr. John Rudley, President
3100 Cleburne Street
Houston, Texas 77004
www.tsu.edu
Public

Wiley College
Dr. Haywood Strickland, President
711 Wiley Avenue
Marshall, Texas 75670
www.wileyc.edu
Private

Virginia

Hampton University
Dr. William R. Harvey, President
Hampton, Virginia 23668
www.hamptonu.edu
Private

Norfolk State University
Dr. Carolyn W. Meyers, President
700 Park Avenue, Suite 520
Norfolk, Virginia 23504
www.nsu.edu
Public

Saint Paul's College
Dr. Robert L. Satcher, Sr., President
115 College Drive
Lawrenceville, Virginia 23868
www.saintpauls.edu
Private

Virginia State University
Dr. Eddie Moore, Jr., President
One Hayden Drive
Petersburg, Virginia 23806
www.vsu.edu
Public

Virginia Union University
Dr. Belinda C. Anderson, President
1500 North Lombardy Street
Richmond, Virginia 23220
www.vuu.edu
Private

Virginia University of Lynchburg
Dr. Ralph Reavis, Sr., President
2058 Garfield Avenue
Lynchburg, Virginia 24501
www.vulonline.us
Private

Virgin Islands

University of The Virgin Islands
Dr. LaVerne Ragster, President
2 John Brewers Bay
Saint Thomas, Virgin Islands 00802
www.uvi.edu
Public

West Virginia

Bluefield State College
Dr. Albert Walker, President
219 Rock Street
Bluefield, West Virginia 24701
www.bluefield.wvnet.edu
Public

West Virginia State University
Dr. Hazo W. Carter, Jr., President
P.O. Box 399
Institute, West Virginia 25112
www.wvstateu.edu
Public

NAFEO BOARD OF DIRECTORS

Joe A. Lee, Chairman
President – Alabama State University

William R. Harvey, Immediate Past Chairman
President – Hampton University

Ernest McNealey, Vice Chairman
President – Stillman College

Dianne Boardley Suber
President - Saint Augustine's College

Walter D. Broadnax
President - Clark Atlanta University

Elnora D. Daniel
President - Chicago State University

Larry L. Earvin
President - Huston-Tillotson College

Mary Evans Sias
President - Kentucky State University

Beverly Hogan
President - Tougaloo College

Edison O. Jackson
President - Medgar Evers College, CUNY

Melvin Johnson
President - Tennessee State University

Trudie Kibbe Reed
President - Bethune Cookman College

Ronald Mason
President - Jackson State University

Ivory Nelson
President - Lincoln University (Pennsylvania)

Ralph Slaughter
President - Southern University System

Thelma Thompson
President - University of Maryland Eastern Shore

Wayne Watson
Chancellor - City Colleges of Chicago

Lezli Baskerville
NAFEO President & CEO - Ex. OFFICIO

NAFEO EXECUTIVE OFFICERS AND STAFF

Executive Officers

Lezli Baskerville, Esq.
President and CEO

Shelia High King
Executive Vice President

Peter G. Parham
Vice President of Strategic Relations

Staff

Gladys Buck
Director of Administration & Finance

Selena Mendy Singleton
Director of Policy, Advocacy, and Government Affairs

Rhonda Davis
Senior Visiting Manager for Federal Programs and White House Initiatives

Lamont Clark
Program Manager

LaNitra Walker Berger
Senior Manager of Research and Policy

Lionel Smith
Research Assistant

Jasmine Jenkins
Internship Coordinator

Derek Simms
Legislative and Legal Assistant